JOURNEY TOWARD

JOURNEY TOWARD WHOLENESS

A Jungian Model
of
Adult Spiritual Growth

Helen Thompson, B.V.M.

PAULIST PRESS
New York / Ramsey

Library of Congress
Catalog Card Number: 81-83184

ISBN: 0-8091-2422-X

Published by Paulist Press
545 Island Road, Ramsey, N.J. 07446

Printed and bound in the
United States of America

CONTENTS

ACKNOWLEDGEMENTS

You—my community of readers—
  may surmise from my title and
  will quickly discover in the text that
    Journey Toward Wholeness
    is an autobiographical essay about
    transitions in adult life.
Those of you who have experienced
being-in-transition
  will immediately recognize that
  turning-points in one's personal journey
    only yield new life and meaning
    when undertaken within the support of
    a loving community of persons.
It is with deep gratitude that
I introduce this support community
  who have nurtured both
  me and my telling of my story—to
    you—my community of readers.

Initially I mention
the Faculty, Staff, and Participants of
  The Institute of Spirituality and Worship
  whose interwoven lives
    formed a fabric of renewal for me
    at the Jesuit School of Theology
    in Berkeley—1978–1979.
I am particularly grateful to
  Jake Empereur, S.J.
    whose vision conceived of the Institute—
  Bob Egan, S.J. and Jim Neafsey

whose own life-journeys shed
light and meaning on mine—
Margaret Dwyer, R.S.C. and Carolyn Glynn, S.P.
and my Reflection Group
who listened so caringly to my story.
It is to Don Gelpi, S.J. and Roy Fairchild
members of the Faculty at
The Graduate Theological Union
that I am most grateful for insights into
the patterns of adult development
and of religious conversion—and
the philosophical framework within which
I interpret religious experience.

Secondly, I acknowledge with gratitude
Meinrad Craighead
whose truly contemplative life is
creatively expressed in
magnificent visual and verbal symbols.
Her recent publication
The Sign of the Tree—
Meditations in Images and Words.
London: Artist House, 1979.
inspired me to inquire about
my using her "Tree of Polarities"
which captures symbolically
the meaning of my message.
Her gracious response
provided me with
an original piece of her work
which I share with you
on the cover of my work.

Finally, I acknowledge with deepest gratitude
those women in my immediate community
whose loving concern for me and my growth
has enabled this painful transition to
yield new life and new meaning—

new meaning which I share *with* you
that it might yield new life *for* you.
Although separated by many miles
I am grateful to
Sheila O'Brien, Peggy Geraghty, and Katrine Johnston
B.V.M.'s who have cared and
who have shared
my vision and my travail.
I am especially grateful for three women
whose lives have touched mine more closely—
Roberdette Burns, B.V.M.
whose faith-filled caring patience
has encouraged me these past few years—
Margaret Thornton, B.V.M.
whose personal vision and loving concern
have inspired me for many years—
my mother Gertrude
whose life at 84 years
continues to support, inspire, and amaze me.

Thanksgiving 1981
Berkeley, California

PROLOGUE

The essay which follows is an autobiographical statement—the result of a five year personal quest. My informal search for meaning has resulted in formalized research. I have searched out and temporarily found a psychological model that encompasses wholistic human growth.

My method of investigation relates directly to the content of the investigation. The search process itself illumines the topic researched. The process describing how human beings achieve meaning relates directly to the product describing how human beings wholistically grow—the outcome of my quest. In this essay the medium also communicates the message.

The method of symbol—the intuitive-holistic mode of consciousness characteristic of the brain's right hemisphere—dominates the initial chapters of the quest. The method of science—the rational analytic mode of consciousness characteristic of the brain's left hemisphere—directs the final chapters. I suggest that all bodies of human knowledge proceed in this manner—the approach of symbol and intuition precedes the approach of science and inference. I suggest that this relationship reflects the pattern basic to the search for human meaning.

My six major resources include individuals from diverse professional, religious, and national backgrounds who use different methodologies to explore apparently dissimilar phenomena within human experience:

Pierre Teilhard de Chardin, a French Jesuit paleontologist, envisioned the phenomenon of human growth within the entire evolutionary process.

C. G. Jung, a Swiss psychoanalyst, departed from Freudian theory, repudiated traditional Protestant Christianity, and developed his own analytic psychology to explain the dynamics and development of the human psyche.

Evelyn Underhill, an English woman, has researched the history and literature of the Christian mystics and presented a psychological map of the mystical way.

William Johnston, a Jesuit from Belfast, teaches in Tokyo where he continues to explore the relationships between the meditation practices and the mystic experience of Eastern religions and those of Christianity.

Erich Neumann, who was born in Berlin and was educated in part by Jung, explored archetypal patterns in world mythologies which characterized the stages in the history of consciousness in the life of humanity as well as the development of consciousness within the individual.

Robert Ornstein, an American psychologist whose work reflects little acquaintance with the Judaic-Christian religious tradition, argues toward a complete psychology of consciousness incorporating the specialized functions of both hemispheres in the brain and for the education of the right brain's intuitive mode of knowing.

The essay which follows attempts to synthesize insights from these six persons and to critically formulate a psychological model of adult spiritual growth. It culminates in an effort to place the model within the context of Donald Gelpi's experienced-based theory of the emergent self. Finally, I suggest several concluding implications for areas of human concern which might be enriched were the model used to illumine them.

CHAPTER I

A PERSONAL QUEST TOWARD UNDERSTANDING HUMAN SPIRITUALITY

Ground of my Being
      Matrix of all living things
            out of which
            my life springs
      becomes my bedrock
            in which is hollowed
            a womb and a tomb
Below weathered cliffs
      in a sheltered cove
            surging waves hallow
            an inner cave.

My ego emerges
      waxing like the moon.
      It submerges my self
            within a
            hollow tomb.
The moon enlarges.
      Cool conscious light
            ascends and

wends its way
through a cloud-studded
night.

Life goes well—
all is calm
and in control.
Rolling waves swell—
a gentle
ebb and flow.
The moon achieves
a lusty glow—
a short-lived show.
It mocks the sun's
setting gold.
The ego's full sail
makes its longest trip
failing to see
the state of its ship.

The moon rises slowly—
darkness begins its reign.
The ego wanes—
life can never
be the same.
Appearances deceived
creating life's lie.
The ego must die
so the self
can arise.
A surging wave
crashes within the cave
merging briny darkness
with inner confusion.

A self—long concealed—
is revealed,

slowly becomes
more real.
A silver disc? Yes
and a shadow
a dark side
a sphere of dust.
Puffs of mist? Yes
but more
a violent inner core.

Fractured facades
fracture this tomb
the self's womb
and nurture
new life.

The full moon wanes
its hidden parts emerge.
Ebbing tides
reveal gifts
long submerged.
Colored clouds fade
mysterious fog
rains on the earth.
Shadow envelops the world.

In a cave confusion
an ego died
was crucified
and entombed.
An inner self rises
violent
broken.
An old tomb
a new womb
in the Ground of my Being.
A hole impaled

by Wholeness
The Hole of Holiness
The Matrix
of
All Living Things.

During the past few months I have told my personal story several
ways. In synopsis form I have enumerated the events of my life and I
have reflected on my relationship to them. In the first version of my
story, I recounted my voyage of discovery. I plotted the path of my
outward journey, reporting those conscious memories which I immediately associated with the events I recalled. With bold strokes I outlined my course across "the first half" of my life.

The second time I told my story in allegory. It narrated the tale of
a shepherd Pan. More to the point, it developed from an experience
of some vivid personal imagery which I wanted to explore. The initial
image presented itself to me in the form of a mandala as I sat one eve-
ning before my prayer candle. Having just owned a painful aspect of
myself, the candle's light, fractured by my tears, cleared and I found
myself floating within an inverted Byzantine dome. At the base? or
top? of this ornate structure, a strong light emerged from a small ap-
erture. I descended into the dome so I could discover the source of
this light. The brilliance emerged from a tiny porthole. I worked my
way into a position so I could look through it. To my amazement I
gazed out onto a magnificent two-part scene which seemed to fill the
whole universe. The full moon shone against a star-filled night sky; sil-
very cumulus clouds separated night from day; undulating waves qui-
etly rose and fell against a rocky coast.

This imagery suggested the setting for the allegory in which Pan
dreamed about his adventure in the cave and his subsequent conver-
sation with Dion, Claudius, and Roland—personifications of the
moon, the clouds and the rocks. I was more than usually fascinated by
this strange tale I had made up. I reread it many times. Gradually I
realized that the story of Pan was not about an isolated painful event
in my mid-life; rather, it was the story of my life. I retold my tale in
another way. The final time I used the free verse form which appears
on subsequent pages.

My interest in understanding my own life story
    has become more academic
        more theoretically oriented.
    I want to understand
        more adequately
        the process of spiritual growth in adult life.
    I want to develop
        a theoretical framework
        that illumines the psychology of spirituality.
    My quest for a wholistic model
        to illuminate adult spiritual growth
        grows out of my experience as
            an educated, professional American woman and
            a member of a Roman Catholic religious congregation.

My "formation" was about equally divided between
    education in a secular context and
    education in a religious context.
        My home life, elementary school years in California and
            my graduate education at Chicago were secular.
        My secondary school years, my notiviate, and
            my scattered undergraduate education were religious.
My "formation" was based—at least implicitly—
    on philosophical positions
    which were conflicting and
        which reflected the widening gap between
        my secular and my religious education.
        My secular education was experientially oriented.
        My religious education was essentially scholastic.
My "formation" produced a symbolically confused sexual identity.
    I was a tomboy but I was not very tough.
    We had a housekeeper who did all the domestic chores
        so both my parents could teach school and
        we could vacation frequently in California's out-of-doors.
We enjoyed the Sierras and camped on the coast.
    My mother reminds me of the mountains—
        a determined woman surmounting obstacles.

My father reminds me of the sea—
    a gentle man rolling with the waves.
I have continually experienced the struggle
    between religious and secular positions
    between experiential and scholastic thought
    between behavior symbolically feminine and
        behavior symbolically masculine.

My personal story
    recounts the tale of a woman
        entrapped in the masculine myth of activity.
I believed that the "real world" was the external one
    which was experienced and explained.
    I gave little value to
    feeling—an obstacle to be surmounted—and
    imagination—only fantasy and therefore "unreal."
I developed professional skills in instruction and administration
    and I used them successfully to construct
    more human environments for learning.
I did a lot of "becoming" and only a little "being."
    Fortunately I was able "to be"
    with my few intimate friends and in the out-of-doors
    driving the back roads of Dubuque County
    skiing Mississippi bluffs and Sierra slopes
    beachcombing sands on the Pacific and the Cape.
    Unfortunately I viewed my "being" activities
    as necessary-for-survival retreats—
    escapes from the "real world of becoming"
    necessitated by weakness.
I discovered one year—
    suddenly and very painfully—
    that the masculine myth of activity
    just does not work!
My professional world and my community life
    collapsed simultaneously.
    At the end of one week at the end of the summer
        I was out of work and
        out of a home.

Since then my journey has been a quest
　　to understand what had happened
　　to the first half of my life and
　　to re-envision the second half of it more wholistically.

The first half of my personal story
　　contains elements which reflect—
　　　　at least from my perspective—
　　not only the unique details of my autobiography.
It also contains elements in the contemporary quest shared
　　　　by members of my religious congregation and
　　　　by many professionally educated American women
　　　　as they seek equality of opportunity
　　　　to use their gifts within the human community.
I trust that the journey I have begun will enable me
　　　　to make sense out of the first half of my life and
　　　　to envision a more meaningful framework
　　　　for the second half of my life.
　　I intend to move toward the creation of a model
　　　　which will provide a psychological understanding
　　　　of the process of adult spiritual growth.
　　I hope that applications of this model
　　　　may illumine the experience of
　　　　other professionally educated
　　　　American women religious and
　　　　all persons seriously concerned about the quality of life
　　　　and wholistic human growth.

CHAPTER II

A JOURNEY TO THE CENTER: A COMPARISON OF TEILHARD AND JUNG

The Stuff of the Universe

In a single phenomenon there is a dual dimension.
　　There is a double aspect
　　　　to the structure of things
　　　　to the stuff of the universe
　　　　to the nature of human beings.

In each phenomenon
　　there is a without
　　　　an exterior which is determinate,
　　　　material, physical, physiological, and
　　there is a within
　　　　an interior which is conscious and spontaneous,
　　　　indeterminate, psychical, psychological.
As the structure of things
　　becomes enriched, more energized, better organized,
the processes in things
　　become centered, better focused, more conscious.[1]

In each phenomenon
　　there is

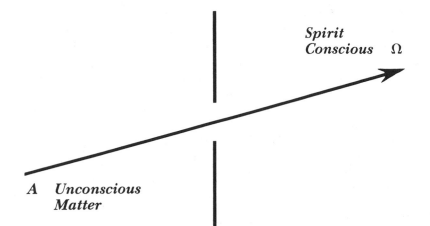

FIGURE 1:
The Evolution of the Human Psyche:
Matter-Becoming Spirit
The Unconscious Becoming Conscious

    matter-becoming-spirit
    a material synthesis and a spiritual completion.
It is the law of complexity-consciousness.[2]
Matter and spirit
    are not "things" or "natures."
    They are simply
        related variables—
    two aspects of the same phenomenon.[3]

Synthesizing the Split-World View

Western civilization has created a split-world view of reality. In contemporary life, the real world is "out there." Success is measured by how well we "make it" out in the "real world." We value achievement and objectivity, science and social class, analysis and responsible activity. Our perception that "reality" is "out there" is the product of our exclusively masculine cultural consciousness.

    The problem is not that we value accomplishment and the atti-

11

tude of scientific analysis. Rather, the problem results from our valuing the products of the rational mind exclusively. We have not only neglected, we have even denied, the reality of a world within. Feeling and instinct, intuition and imagination have been diverted from the mainstream of human life, relegated to isolated havens inhabited by artists, poets, mystics, and a few highly creative individuals whose synthetic thought may eventually influence the direction of the cultural current. Teilhard and Jung are two such men whose insights into the phenomenon of human beings have recognized our polarized world view. Each in his own way has helped restore the "within" and to integrate the "feminine" into human consciousness.

For Teilhard the human element is a phenomenon with a double aspect—a without and a within. The human person is matter-becoming-spirit. In the course of development, as the external dimension complexifies, the inner dimension intensifies. Jung suggests an interesting analogy. For him the phenomenon of the human element can be represented as a psyche, a self-regulating system structured in opposites. A human person evolves as that which was unconscious becomes conscious. Matter becomes spirit—the unconscious becomes conscious: these are two symbolic representations expressing the dual dimension in the phenomenon of man and in the phenomenon of the human psyche.

Energy Propels Matter-Becoming-Spirit

Energy has two components.[4]
    External tangential energy
        links what is like
        in complexity and consciousness.[5]
    External energy accounts for
        our socio-industrial arrangements,
        our service and maintenance activity, and
        the process of our individualization.

    Internal radial energy
        lures life forward
        toward greater complexity and consciousness.[6]
    Internal energy motivates

discovery, exploration, education,
passion, compassion, communion, and
the process of our individuation.

External energy conceals itself
in the formation of conditioned behavior.
Internal energy reveals itself
in the transformation of the person.[7]

Energy propels life forward
an unfolding without
an enfolding within
the twofold process
of continuity and change.

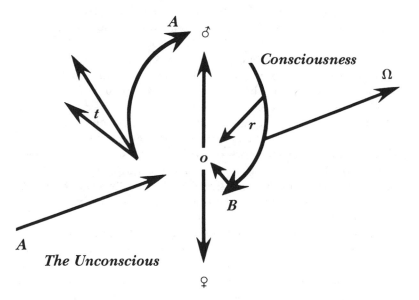

FIGURE 2:
The Human Psyche Evolves within Two Polar Tensions:
External (t) Energy and Internal (r) Energy
The Unconscious and the Conscious

Psychic Energy and Personal Growth

Teilhard and Jung use "energy" to symbolize the force that propels human evolution. Psychic energy directs and motivates the human personality; it is the dynamism of the life process within the psychic sphere. For Jung[8] psychic energy can be transformed or displaced, but not destroyed—the law of conservation. Psychic energy is generated by the polar tensions and intercourse between the "opposites" which structure the psyche. This second law, the law of opposites, includes a variety of polarities—the conscious and various complexes of the unconscious: thinking and feeling, sensation and intuition; separation, union; activity, receptivity. "Opposites" represent "the other" and hence have become identified symbolically with sexual polarity—the masculine and the feminine.

Polarities should not be confused with polarization. A polarity suggests a single phenomenon with a double aspect; a continuum with two poles; a union of reconcilable opposites. Polarization suggests dichotomized, separate entities, related but rent. Psychic energy is generated by polarity not by polarization.

Teilhard's images of tangential and radial energy suggest an interesting polarity. Consider an object in curvilinear motion. Tangential energy directs the object outward, straightening the path on which it travels. Radial energy directs the object inward toward the center from which it emerged. Tangential energy tends toward an outward point widening the curve; radial energy tends toward an inward point centering the curve. If the polar tension between these energies were equal, they would function as centripetal and centrifugal action and the object would travel in a circle. However, if tangential energy were stronger initially and radial energy stronger at a subsequent time, the object would travel in a spiral.

The human psyche is evolving within the play of two polar tensions—tangential and radial energy and the conscious and the unconscious. Development can be described as the movement from the unconscious, undifferentiated beginning toward a subsequent point of personal, integrated wholeness. During "the first half" of life, the ego emerges and then moves toward greater conscious control; the outward influence of tangential energy predominates. During "the second half" of life, elements of the unconscious emerge seeking integration; the inward influence of radial energy predominates. Polar tension creates psychic energy which propels the process of growth.

Evolution and Involution

That which has existed within
    obscurely and in a primordial way
        unfolds into greater complexity and
        ramifies into a multiplicity of parts.[9]

The element approaches a critical point,
    confronts a crisis,
    crosses a threshold
        irreversibly.[10]

That which is new
    yet contains what has been
        enfolds upon its center and
        concentrates into new unity and consciousness.[11]

What has been
    is now and will be
        changed but
        in continuity with its primordial self.[12]

In human evolution
    an infant or adolescent or adult
        develops skills
        gains mastery and
        becomes comfortably satisfied.
    But satisfaction soon wanes.

The individual
    is jolted, is shaken, is prodded by
        enemies or events without;
    is impelled, is directed, is drawn forward by
        a principle within

to break with the collective framework
which has imprisoned him.[13]

In human involution
    an infant or adolescent or adult
        confronts a critical point, crosses a threshold
        and enters a deeper state of consciousness.[14]

Thresholds as Death-Rebirth Encounters

Teilhard's understanding of evolution as a directed movement through a series of critical thresholds can be compared to Jung's stages of psychic development through a series of death-rebirth encounters. Initially the individual confronts the threshold of physical birth, that traumatic event which abruptly separates the infant from the comfortable world of the womb. Although physically separate, the newborn child is psychically undifferentiated from its mother. Symbolically it remains at-one-with the nourishing flesh that bore it. The individual lives in a primitive union with nature.

During childhood the ego begins to emerge becoming aware of its own autonomy and separateness but still unable to sever itself from the nurturance of "parental" support. Unfortunately psychic childhood is not a matter of chronological development. Underdeveloped egos, dependent upon external authority and expectations, may continue to reside in physically mature adults. The threshold of psychic adolescence is crossed when the emerging ego asserts its authority and severs itself from the psychic parental framework that nurtured, supported, and gave it shape. It is the first bold act of masculine independence destined to be repeated throughout life because the psychological power of parental authority lives on within the individual's personal unconscious. Symbolically represented by Jung as a complex, the contents of the personal unconscious secretly imprison and may frequently threaten the conscious ego during adult life. Unlike the threshold of physical birth which is crossed irreversibly and only once, the second threshold is a series of critical points, spread across life, each one of which is crossed irreversibly.

The next stage of development begins in mid-life as the individual becomes aware of and listens to the contents of his world within.

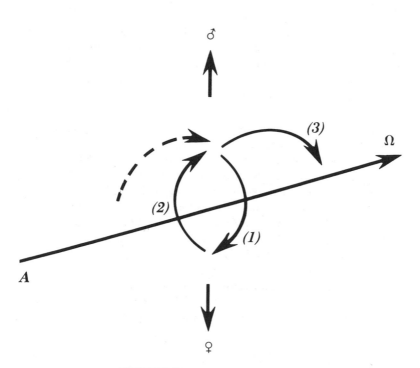

FIGURE 3:
Crossing Critical Thresholds is a
Threefold Process:
(1) A Period of Disintegration
(2) A Period of Painful Transition
(3) A Period of Integration

He begins to acknowledge the "complexes" clothed in the material of his personal life. He gradually recognizes that, beneath these personal contents which are unique to himself, there lie struggles common to all human beings. At the core of his personal concerns he uncovers mysteries universal to human experience symbolically represented as "archetypes." A personal, yet universal, new inner world discloses itself revealing depths to his psyche heretofore unrealized by the conscious ego. Elements from the collective unconscious or objective psyche begin to emerge. Although king in the conscious realm, the ego comes to recognize a new center, another inner principle that directs and integrates the individual's life from within. The third threshold, again a series of critical points, is crossed as the ego surrenders to this other inner principle, for Jung, the Self. Mediated through the contents of the unconscious, its "complexes" and "archetypes," the Self, that inner principle which has existed obscurely and in a primordial way, emerges into the person's consciousness. The Self directs the person's life in a new way; it integrates elements from the conscious and the unconscious, from the outer and the inner world, capturing the energy released by these recognized polar tensions. The newly realized energy intensifies consciousness and energizes life's activity. The individual is drawn forward by a principle from within to break with the frameworks that imprison him and to consciously act with a spontaneity that wells up from the depths of his centered Self.

Physical birth is a death to the comfort of prenatal existence. Each autonomous act of the emerging ego kills the authority of the "parents" which formed it. Consciousness is transformed as the ego surrenders to the Self; every subsequent threshold crossed tolls a knell to the exclusive control of ego consciousness over the activities of life.

Individualization and Personalization

If the individual's growth
    is exclusively through conditioning
        from without
    his behavior hardens, his life atrophies,
        his consciousness extraverts
        contracting into automatic, rigid activity.

Conditioned by the culture which imprisons him,
    an individualized human element
        is regarded as an accessory,
        his uniqueness is sacrificed.
    The individual identifies with a role defined by society.
        The self grows weaker
        sapped by demands others place upon it.

Identified with the group without
    but isolated within,
        the conditioned psychic center is passed over and ignored.
External conditioning alone results in rigid responses
    paralyzing, ultimately destroying, the unique inner self.[15]

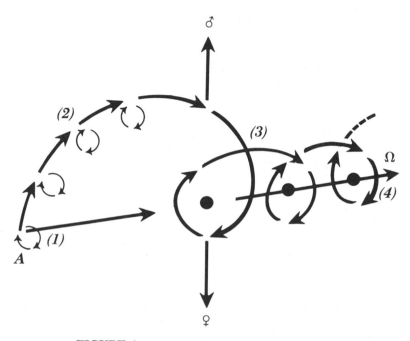

FIGURE 4:
The Stages of Psychic Development through a
Series of Death-Rebirth Encounters:
(1) Physical Birth—Death to Prenatal Comfort
(2) Ego Development—Death to Childhood
Dependence
(3) Emergence of the Self—Death to Ego
Control
(4) Transcendence of This Life—Death to
This Life

If the individual's growth
    is supple, open to nourishment
        from within
    his behavior remains flexible, his life advances,
        his consciousness introverts,
            expanding toward more concentrated spontaneity.

Having penetrated new interior space,
    a personalized reflective center,
        establishes more coherent, better organized
        perceptions of reality around him.
The personalized center plumbs the depths
    of his interior vortex
        which grows deeper as it sucks up fluid
        at the heart of which it was born.[16]

The ego merges with the self
    in the measure to which
        it takes everything else into its self.
In internal transformation, the person becomes different
    yet remains the same—true to his unique inner self.[17]

Individualization and Individuation

Teilhard distinguishes between the process of individualization and the process of personalization. Jung identifies the final stage of psychic development as the process of individuation. I suggest that in the evolution of the human psychic element, during the first half of life, external energy forms the ego as the individual is socialized; the process of individualization predominates. Individualization becomes an aberration when it is the only stage in psychic development. Unfortunately socialization in contemporary life is frequently the only aspect of adult growth.

Conditioned by our culture, we acquire the values and attitudes espoused by the group with which we identify. Our ghetto may be urban or suburban; our work may be industrial, governmental, or academic; it matters little if we respond only to the expectations of others, if we only fill a role, if we only identify exclusively with the "persona" we present to the outside world. An organization person performs a specialized function in a bureaucratic society; the psychic center is passed over and ignored. Conditioning from without paralyzes and ultimately destroys the unique inner self. Such is the aberration of individualization.

I further suggest that during the second half of life, internal energy transforms the socialized individual into a personalized self; Teilhard's process of personalization or Jung's process of individuation predominates. In admitting the contents of the personal and collective unconscious, the ego is nourished from within expanding its consciousness ever deeper toward its own psychic center. The self penetrates deeper into its own interior vortex drawing inspiration, vitality, and direction from its own unique core, the matrix from which life springs.

Sexuality in Hominized Form

Centered human selves
    influence and penetrate
    other reflective centers.
        Radial energy relates
    what is deepest
    within human beings
        so as
        to complete and
        to fulfill them.

Love completes
    as it unites.
    Union differentiates.
By coinciding with another
        we penetrate further
            the center of our selves.[18]

In hominized form
    sexuality functions
    in a unique way.
        The radial energy of love

synthesizes the two principles
male and female
in the building of
the human personality.
The complete human being
is a duality comprising
masculine and feminine
together.[19]

In the phenomenon of each person
there is a dual dimension—
matter-becoming-spirit
the masculine residing with the feminine.[20]

Sexuality and Personal Integration

For Teilhard it is through radial energy that one reflective center influences and penetrates other centered selves. The attraction of love relates what is deepest-within-one to what is deepest-within-another so as to complete and fulfill both selves. In human form sexuality synthesizes the individual by integrating the masculine with the feminine within as well as without. The complete human being is a duality comprising the masculine and the feminine together.

Jung posited that within each individual there exists an "other." There exists a contrasexual principle. For men, the anima symbolically represents the feminine principle; for women, the animus symbolically represents the masculine principle. The contents of the contrasexual principle are acquired from close associations with persons of the opposite sex who are significant in personal development.

The feminine principle contains elements concerned with life as an unpremediated, spontaneous, natural phenomenon of involvement and relatedness with others. Characteristics of the feminine principle include tenderness and sensitivity; deviousness and seduction; feeling and receptivity; creative containing and yielding. The masculine principle contains elements concerned with life as a consciously premediated, directed phenomenon of initiative, independence, and separateness from others. Characteristics of the masculine principle include discipline and analysis; aggressive assertiveness,

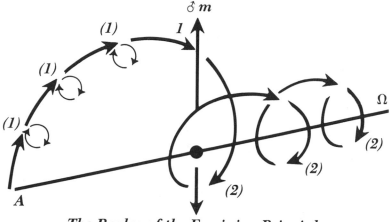

The Realm of the Masculine Principle
♂ m

The Realm of the Feminine Principle
♀ f

FIGURE 5:
The Realm and the
Behavior of the Countersexual
Principles in the Human
Psyche Become Integrated

(m) **Conscious Mediator, Independence**
(f) **Unpremediated, Relatedness**
(1) **Initiative, Creative Construction**
(2) **Creative Containing, Yielding**

search for meaning; discrimination and judgment; initiative and creative construction. The contrasexual principle functions to mediate the contents of the collective unconscious to the conscious ego.

Sexual polarity is an experience of the within as well as of the without. Just as we discover unguessed depths within ourselves as a result of outwardly relating to persons of the opposite sex, so too, in relating to the inner "person" of our anima or animus, we become connected with our inner contrasexual principle of femininity or masculinity. We become connected to our objective psyche and its archetypal images of the masculine and the feminine by becoming aware of the personal contents of our contrasexual complex.

By embracing otherness, by capturing the energy released by the union of sexual opposites, by integrating elements of the unconscious into the conscious, we become more distinctively our selves. Love, of self and of others, completes as it unites. Union differentiates.

The Personal and The Universal

In the human phenomenon
    consciousness enfolds everything,
        at least partially
    upon itself.

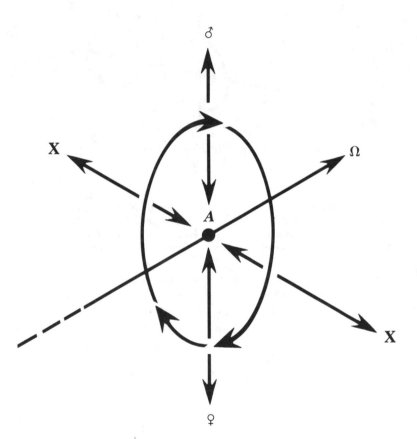

FIGURE 6:
In the Individuated Self the Personal (A) and
the Universal (x), the One (A) and the Many (x)
Culminate Simultaneously in Human Solidarity

Consciousness centers itself
    upon itself, and
        becomes more associated
        with the All.
The personal and the universal
    grow in the same direction
        culminating simultaneously
        in one another.[21]

Personal Integration and Human Solidarity

Jung's archetype of the Self expresses psychic wholeness and totality. It is the center but also the circumference since it embraces both the conscious and the unconscious elements of the psyche. The Self resides at the center of the total psyche just as the ego dominates the center of the conscious mind. However, the Self's organizing activity is never fully integrated because the unconscious remains an inexhaustible depth within which an undetermined amount of material lies hidden, material common to all human experience.

The individuated Self incorporates within itself what it personally experiences of the many, of the human condition, from without. The individuated Self incorporates within itself contents presented by the objective psyche within—contents common to the universal struggles of all human beings. The personal and the universal culminate simultaneously in one another within the individuated Self.

The Christian Phenomenon

In the Christian phenomenon
    God immerses himself
        in the heart of the matter
        becoming a human element.

Christ directs and animates
    the evolutionary process—
        the expansion of consciousness—
        into which he inserts himself.

The Risen Lord aggregates to himself
    the total psyche—the total psychism of the earth.
His Redeeming Incarnation
    gathers and transforms all
        into himself—the center of centers.

The individual Christian opus—the work of human works—
    is to establish an absolutely original center
        in which the universe reflects itself
        in a unique inimitable way.[22]
These original centers—
    Christ the Alpha—
        are our very Selves which
        Christ the Omega must reclaim.[23]

Toward Some Initial Conclusions and a Tentative Hypothesis

The preceding comparative analysis of Teilhard's evolution of the human element and Jung's development of the human psyche suggests several initial conclusions about a developmental model of spiritual growth.

1. The evolution of the human psyche moves in a predictable direction. The undifferentiated material world of the infant moves toward greater consciousness and the differentiated spiritual world of the mature adult. Figure 1 suggests that matter is becoming spirit; that the unconscious is becoming conscious.

2. The human psyche is propelled to grow through energy generated by the tensions created by polar opposites. Figure 2 suggests two such polar tensions: (1) the tension created by an extraverted orientation moving the individual toward the external world and by an introverted orientation moving the individual toward the internal world, and (2) the tension between the conscious and the unconscious.

3. Human growth occurs as the individual crosses a critical threshold. Figure 3 illustrates this process as including three stages: (1) a period of disintegration, a separation from the former ways, (2) a period of painful transition and awkward behavior, and (3) a period of integration around a new way of organizing one's life. The former

ways become meaningless or inadequate. What was, can no longer be; but, what is to come, is not yet present. When the future cannot be envisioned, the present is experienced as darkness. As new possibilities dawn, the psyche begins to reconstruct itself around more meaningful, adequate ways, around a new center of consciousness. These three stages suggest the process of conversion.

4. Between the initial threshold crossed, physical birth, and the final threshold of physical death, the life span can be conceived of as a series of death-rebirth encounters or conversions. Figure 4 also suggests that at some point during the middle part of adult life the individual experiences a major crisis which, if confronted and successfully crossed, transforms the direction of his or her life. Although adolescence and young adulthood consist of a series of critical thresholds, the major thrust of the first half of life is in the direction of greater consciousness and control. During the first half of life, the ego develops; it may also become inflated. With the mid-life crisis the ego is deflated. Although the process of disintegration is painful and frightening to the ego relinquishing control, the deeper levels of the psyche are freed to emerge. During the second half of life, the self emerges, again, through a series of conversions.

5. "Opposites" represent "the other" and hence have become identified symbolically with sexual polarity. Consciousness has become associated symbolically with the realm of the masculine; the unconscious with the realm of the feminine. Initiating, constructing, conscious behavior has been associated symbolically with the masculine; containing, yielding, spontaneous behavior with the feminine. Figure 5 suggests that during the first half of life ego development tends in the direction of the masculine especially to the degree that the rational ego becomes inflated, that is, cut off from its opposite: feeling, imagination, the unconscious. The mid-life crisis conversion turns the psyche in the direction of the feminine principle. Figure 5 also suggests that the first phase of the conversion cycle can be characterized symbolically as feminine, that is, a letting go and a becoming receptive. The third phase of the conversion cycle can be characterized symbolically as masculine, a building up and a re-envisioning. The two "halves of life" and the two phases of the conversion cycle suggest an alterneity between the masculine and the feminine as an essential component of growth toward integration.

27

6. Finally, Figure 6 suggests two things: first that the individuated self has reconciled and uses alternately the sexual polarities just previously discussed and, secondly, that the individuated self has reconciled and uses alternately the introverted and extraverted polarities. Independence and solitude co-exist with involvement and relatedness. Within the individuated self personal human concerns are united with universal human concerns. The one unites with the many in human solidarity.

Unfortunately, Western culture does little to facilitate adult growth toward integration, a process dependent upon the reconciliation of realms and behaviors associated with both the masculine and the feminine. In fact, our exclusively masculine cultural consciousness envisions a dual world of polarization. Matter is separate from spirit. The conscious is rent from the unconscious. The masculine belongs only to male persons; the feminine to female persons. These are "things," distinct entities; not related variables, two aspects of the same phenomenon. The "without" is valued; the "within" is denied. Consequently, interiority and all associated with it—feelings, imagery, symbolic meaning, mythic thinking, as well as behaviors such as "being," receptivity, and surrender—have been seriously neglected. The six conclusions generated by a comparative analysis of Teilhard and Jung and viewed against our patriarchal cultural milieu suggest a tentative hypothesis concerning a model for adult spiritual growth toward integration.

Adult human growth toward integration
   will proceed wholistically
   only if
      the neglected realm of interiority
         symbolically associated with the feminine
      is dialectically reconciled with
      the dominant realm of exteriority
         symbolically associated with the masculine.

CHAPTER III

A MAP OF THE MYSTICAL WAY
A COMPARISON OF
UNDERHILL AND JOHNSTON

The mystical journey—
a psychological and a spiritual experience—is
a purging of the ego and
a preparation of the self,
a movement to higher levels of consciousness, and
a unification with the deeper Self
which touches the transcendental order.[1]

The mystic moves through
a series of oscillations between
states of pain and states of pleasure
Conversion—Awakening
Discipline—Enlightenment
Surrender—Union.[2]
In the beginning of the mystic way
the individual
turns from a vision of reality
viewed exclusively as a product of perception,
breaks with this illusory world of the senses, and
awakens to a new, embryonic consciousness
of divine reality.

Awakening is accompanied by
an experience of joy.

Humbled and awed
by the possibilities which have been revealed,
the individual
retreats into the "cell of self-knowledge" and
labors to adjust to what he envisions
by stripping away obstacles and
by purifying the senses.
Purgation is a state of pain and effort.

Remade during a period of darkness
the individual opens his eyes
on a world still natural,
but no longer illusory.
Illumination brings a vision of
the beauty, the majesty, the divinity
of the living World of Becoming.
Divine Reality is seen as coming
not from some far off spiritual country,
but arising gently from the very heart of things.
Illumination is a contemplative state—
a state of happiness and of light.

Abandoned by many who have traveled this far,
a few descend into the depths of a new night.
The will is cleansed—
the ego surrenders its control.
The spirit is purified—
the very center of I-hood is purged.
The dark night of self-surrender is
a spiritual crucifixion,
a state of great desolation.

At the end of the mystic way
the individual
having surrendered I-hood in its entirety

is drawn into the World of Being
which the World of Becoming had revealed,
is at-one-with the Absolute, and
finds true life hidden in God.
    Union is a state characterized by
        peaceful joy,
        enhanced powers,
        increased activity, and
        intense certitude.[3]

From her exhaustive research of Christian mystical literature, Evelyn Underhill has provided us with a map of the mystic's journey as well as a description of the processes undertaken or undergone by the mystical traveler. In describing the terrain through which the mystic travels, she identifies five—I suggest, six—states which occur in a predictable order. Awakening, Purgation, and Self-Surrender identify the kinds of painful separations and losses the individual undergoes or undertakes during the dis-integrating period of change; Awakening, Illumination, and Union identify the new levels of consciousness around which the individual integrates his life. These states of pain and pleasure alternate, the painful state preparing the way for the pleasurable state. In the course of her descriptive profile of the mystic way, Underhill alludes to apparent paradoxes—polarities which become more completely reconciled at each new level of consciousness: the surface and the suprasensible consciousness, the World of Becoming and the World of Being, Transcendence and Immanence. With bold strokes, I shall outline the map of the mystical way by describing (1) the three successive levels of consciousness and (2) the three successively more painful periods of purgation. At a later time I shall deal with several polarities suggested by the apparent paradoxes which appear in the literature of the mystics.

The mystical way is a journey which is at once psychological and spiritual, a process that moves toward deeper levels of consciousness and greater degrees of freedom. I would prefer to describe the journey of the Christian mystic as the growth of the psyche toward greater integration informed by faith in the God who reveals himself in Jesus and in the power of his Spirit. I believe this statement reflects

31

Underhill's intention when, in 1910, she wrote for a world whose primary ideology espoused a dichotomy between the spiritual and the psychological, between the sensible and the mystical. The prevailing thought of her time did not recognize matter and spirit, the unconscious and the conscious, as being dual aspects of the same phenomenon. I sense that like her contemporaries, Jung and Teilhard, Underhill did intuit these relationships but she lacked both the philosophical and the psychological language to describe them. Moreover, she lacked a readership that would understand them. The problem of language makes an analysis of Underhill somewhat difficult since she addresses an implicitly scholastic theological Christian world which only understood human behavior in terms of faculty psychology. At the risk of introducing error in interpretation, I have chosen to paraphrase, in more contemporary terms, what I sense to be Underhill's meaning.

Successively Deeper Levels of Consciousness: Awakening, Enlightenment, Union

In describing the state of Awakening, Underhill quotes E. T. Starbuck's explanation of conversion. "The larger world consciousness now (presses) in on the individual consciousness. . . . His life becomes swallowed up in a larger whole."[4] The individual's center of interest shifts from a perception of reality that is limited to the surface world of the senses and the field of consciousness is remade about a perception of reality which sees the divine contained within. A sense of the transcendental is awakened and the experience is joyful.

Having experienced the pain of purgation, which will be described below, the self emerges able to apprehend another order of reality. This new consciousness is a deeper, intuitional knowledge; an enlightenment and a certitude about God and the individual's relationship to God. Illumination is experienced by the mystics in three ways: (1) a joyous apprehension of God, a deep sense of dwelling in his presence, (2) a clarity of vision in regard to his action in the phenomenal world, and (3) an increase in the energy of the new self. Those who have experienced Illumination indicate that its symbolic name is really descriptive. They experience a kind of radiance or a flooding of the personality with new light. In Illumination the self becomes conscious that the world he experiences is a living reality, the vast arena of divine creativity in which the individual is immersed. Illumination is a contemplative state; it is experienced as happiness. Many persons travel no further.[5]

Union is the final establishment of that higher form of consciousness which has struggled for supremacy during the whole of the mystical way. The ego having surrendered its control over life, the deepest, richest levels of personality attain consciousness and freedom. The self is remade, transformed into a unified whole. With the termination of stress, power is liberated for new purposes. Union can only be described metaphorically. Some mystics express it as *deification*—a transfusion of the self by God's self, a new order of life, so high and so harmonious, that it can only be called divine. Others describe it as a *spiritual marriage*—the conscious intimate sharing of an inflowing personal life. As a consequence of Union, the mystic is infused with new life that mediates increased activity and creativity.[6]

Successively More Painful Periods of Purgation: Conversion, Discipline, Surrender

In the discussion above, I suggested that there are six stages, not five, in the mystical way implied in Underhill's composite map. I am suggesting that Awakening is in fact a twofold process, a turning away from an old way and a becoming aware of a new way. I suggest that the first period of separation, which may or may not be painful, is explicitly addressed by E. T. Starbuck in his explanation of conversion which, he says, is "primarily an unselfing. The first birth of the individual is into his own little world. He is controlled by the deep-seated instincts of self-preservation and self-enlargement. . . . The universe is organized around his own personality as a centre."[7] A conversion may begin with a single abrupt experience or it may be a gradual process, unmarked by any definite crisis. It may be imposed from without or it may develop from within.[8] In either case, I contend that "the Awakening of the Self to a consciousness of divine reality" is in contrast to a prior way of being; it is first a turning from—a letting-go of—the exclusive control of "the instincts of self-preservation and self-enlargement." So much for what may be merely the two sides of the same coin. I make the point, however, to indicate that a very real form of conscious life existed prior to the initial awakening. For some persons, the form of life may have characterized the entire "first half of their life."

The second period, Purgation, includes a twofold process: detachment and mortification. Detachment is a removal of obstacles that inhibit growth; the unbinding of the fetters that hold us. We seek to free ourselves from the need to possess and to be freed from the things which possess us. Mortification is the exercise of new modes of behavior, the practice of skills that cut new paths and establish new habits. Death to the old ways is often a stormy matter, but its purpose is not death but new life.[9]

The final period of pain, Surrender, or the Dark Night of the Soul, is experienced by the few who pass beyond the state of Illumination. This mystic death is the last painful break with the life of illusion. The individual is torn from the world to which the intellect and senses correspond—the World of Becoming—and is thrust into the World of Being which at first can only be experienced as a wilderness of darkness.[10] In this period of chaos, the destruction of the old equilibrium and the construction of a new, unfamiliar world occur simultaneously. The individual's sense of there being something supremely wrong translates to the surface conscious in any of several forms. (1) It seems as though God, who had once shown himself, has now deliberately withdrawn his presence. (2) The pain of darkness is less a deprivation of light but rather a new, dreadful kind of lucidity. (3) The individual experiences emotional enervation, callousness, boredom. (4) The individual experiences a mental lethargy, a dullness which extends to ordinary mental activity. In the Dark Night of the Soul, the self ceases to be "its own centre and circumference."[11] It is prepared for a final state of union with the Other.

Underhill's map of the mystic way, cumbersome though its language may be, provides a blueprint against which William Johnston's more recent searches into the science of meditation can be compared. Therefore, we turn to his explanation of the expansion of consciousness through deeper levels of prayer and to the insights depth psychology and Eastern forms of meditation shed on the way of contemplation.

The Science of Meditation

The mystical way is a perilous journey.
    It begins with an initial awakening.
    The individual
        enters a new state of awareness—
    he filters out the superficial, wordy rational consciousness
    and sinks into a deeper, silent intuitive consciousness.[12]

The journey continues inward
    along the road to ecstasy.
    Through successively more profound states of prayer
        the prayer of quiet,
        the prayer of union, and
        the prayer of transforming union
    increasingly more powerful uprisings of
        the spirit embedded in the mind and heart,
        the spiritual energies found in the Self,
        the Spirit of Jesus dwelling within
    flow into the heart and
    expand the consciousness.[13]

The life of man is a process of spiritualization
    which reaches its climax
        in the adult processes of aging and death.
    It is a foretaste of the resurrection
        the death of the old man,
        the birth of the new.[14]

Finally the mystic turns outward and
    returns to the market place.
    The discriminating consciousness of the ego
        a product of the left hemisphere of the brain
        at work in the world of becoming—
            the world of business and science and scholarship
    surrenders to and alternates with
    the undifferentiated consciousness of the Self
        a product of the right hemisphere of the brain

at home in the world of being—
the world of art and play and contemplation.[15]
With these inner polarities reconciled
the mystic finds final enlightenment by
a return to
the turbulence of action,
the active service of Christ's humanity,
participatory activity in the cosmic Christ.[16]

The life cycle has run its full circle.
The first journey is outward—
to the world of becoming
of conscious control and activity
The subsequent journey is inward—
to the world of being
of surrender, receptivity, and reconciliation.
The final journey is outward
to the world of contemplative activity
undertaken and undergone
by an enlightened Self
envisioning its Self and the World
as participating in infused Divine Activity.

Insights into the Processes of Prayer and Purgation

It is not surprising that William Johnston's description of the journey of the mystic follows a path similar to the map outlined by Evelyn Underhill. However, with the advantage of an additional half century of exploration into the depths of the psyche and experimental research in the behavioral sciences, neither is it surprising that Johnston makes several suggestions that might aid the individual serious about spiritual growth along the way toward deeper levels of contemplative prayer.

The Initiate is invited to practice relaxation that disconnects the control of the rational ego.[17] The physical relaxation of muscles in the forehead, the jaws and throat and the anus produces a desirable effect. The rhythm and monotony of repeated mantras, the visual imagery of mandalas or objects such as candle flames or flowers which focus attention passively, the process of listening attentively to every sound are techniques that limit the processes of the rational consciousness and force the mind to work vertically downward. With the mind silenced, a whole area of psychic life, ordinarily dormant, is opened up. Images, visual and auditory, can emerge from what the Western mystics have called "the interior senses." In a somewhat different, but related, vein, it should be noted that the experience of intimate love creates a level of awareness and an expansion of the mind that allows for communication at the deeper level of the intuitive consciousness. In fact, all efforts to enter deeper levels of contemplative prayer must originate and be conducted in the context of a love which seeks union with the Other.[18]

The practice of meditation techniques engages the initiate in a new way of being, one of passive concentration which allows for the discharge of passive energy. Passive energy may be something akin to a vehicle for the activity of the Spirit of Jesus. In Christian meditation,

> one goes beyond discursive reasoning and yet remains alert and aware. Here is the core of passive energy. It is found in a state of consciousness where the mind does not go out to an object in order to analyze it in a discursive way. Rather does it take in the whole to "contemplate" (literally "gaze upon") and identify with it. Passive energy belongs to the intuitive way of thinking just as active energy belongs to the discursive. Both are necessary for full human development.[19]

Christian contemplation is the answer to a call, the response to a vision. It is the experience of being loved and of loving at the most profound level of psychic life and of spirit. "So deep is the call and so interior is the response that a new level of awareness is opened" and the individual "enters into a changed environment."[20]

However, with the opening of these new psychic areas, areas in the unconscious, "goblins and ghosts" arise as well as "saints and angels." Repressed negative feelings, fear, guilt, and anger, raise their threatening heads, parental scripts and the voices of the obstreperous "child" shout for a hearing. By exposing these inner demons to the healing power of the Spirit and by experiencing, then embracing as one's own, the inner powers of darkness, the individual is liberated from their possessive control. In an act of repentance, the individual forgives and is forgiven; self-hatred is replaced by a healing self-love; alienated parts of the psyche are reconciled with each other and a more integrated personality emerges.[21] Some have suggested that this confrontation with the shadow is the experience of the Dark Night of the Senses.[22]

But detachment from the instincts and feelings and desires which possess us is not sufficient. The ultimate test demands that we surrender our conscious ways of knowing, our way of controlling. "Conceptual knowledge is a way of mastery that must be abandoned in favor of a non-conceptual knowledge, a whole new mode of knowing and loving which goes into the silence of the cloud or the dark night."[23] The ego, put together during the first half of life, is taken apart in the Dark Night of the Spirit.

In addition to these insights which parallel the process of mystical growth described by Underhill, Johnston suggests that intimacy and sexuality not only bear a direct relationship to the mystical experience but they also illumine both the process of purgation and that of loving union. Contemplation which goes beyond thought and imagery and penetrates the inner core of silence is an arch-enemy of both conscious and unconscious clinging. It frees the individual from the tyranny of his complexes by entering the murky depths of the personal unconscious with its cleansing power. Freed from clinging and possessiveness, the individual can perceive and relate to others, as the other is, not as the individual would have him be. Non-attachment does not establish intimacy, but rather it creates the conditions for it. Intimacy results when two persons dwell within each other; their personalities do not merge; rather, it is an experience of indwelling. Genuine human intimacy illustrates Teilhard's principle that union differentiates. A loving relationship achieved through non-attachment is the kind of union that enables the individuals to find their true selves.[24] However, "non-attachment is a painful process in which the deep caverns of the psyche are purified from jealousy, hatred, possessiveness, anger and selfishness."[25] It can easily be considered among the ascetic disciplines.

Vertical meditation leads to a remarkable control of sexuality. The non-attachment which penetrates the caverns of the psyche liberates the individual from the unconscious fears and traumatic anxieties frequently associated with sexuality and giving of one's self to another. With this liberation comes a powerful self mastery which enables persons to express their love sexually when appropriate or to refrain from the physical expression of it when circumstances so demand. Johnston borrows from Viktor Frankl who claims that in a genuine love relationship, one is moved at the depths of his spiritual core by the partner's spiritual core. All genuine love, enacted at the depths of one's being, which that core opened up through meditation, can be considered a mystical experience.[26]

Finally Johnston refers to Teilhard's idea that the masculine-feminine relationship unleases the energy that builds the cosmos, stimulating the thrust of life toward more fullness of being. Woman, he claims, leads man out of his cramping isolation and points the way to a universal love of involvement.[27] As a woman, I suggest that man leads woman away from her cramping involvements and into a liberating personal solitude. While it is the experience of many men and women that they are actually inspired by loving relationships with persons of the opposite sex, I suggest that these words also possess a symbolic meaning that can be applied to the masculine and feminine principles within persons of both sexes.

It will be recalled that "opposites" represent "the other" and hence have become identified symbolically with sexual polarity. Moreover, according to Jung, psychic energy is generated by the tensions between polarities. Therefore, it is appropriate to examine more closely the several polarities implied by both Underhill and Johnston in their descriptions of the mystical journey.

Apparent Paradoxes: The Principle of Polarity

Five of the most obvious polarities which relate directly to the path of the mystic are illustrated in Figure 7. I have included matter and spirit; the unconscious and the conscious; the rational consciousness and the intuitive consciousness; periods of pain and states of pleasure; and non-attachment in a loving relationship. Each of these finds a form of reconciliation during the mystical way.

However, Underhill discloses another paradox which underlies the mystic's description of the mystical experience. The literature reveals that the divine reality tends to be perceived in two distinct

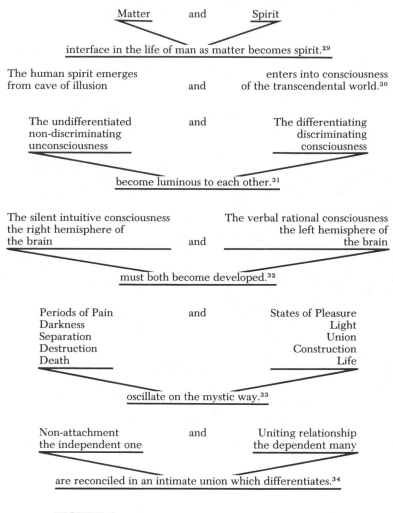

Matter   and   Spirit

interface in the life of man as matter becomes spirit.[29]

The human spirit emerges   enters into consciousness
from cave of illusion   and   of the transcendental world.[30]

The undifferentiated   and   The differentiating
non-discriminating   discriminating
unconsciousness   consciousness

become luminous to each other.[31]

The silent intuitive consciousness   The verbal rational consciousness
the right hemisphere of   the left hemisphere of
the brain   and   the brain

must both become developed.[32]

Periods of Pain   and   States of Pleasure
Darkness   Light
Separation   Union
Destruction   Construction
Death   Life

oscillate on the mystic way.[33]

Non-attachment   and   Uniting relationship
the independent one   the dependent many

are reconciled in an intimate union which differentiates.[34]

FIGURE 7:
Five Polarities, Identified by Underhill and Johnston, That Are Reconciled on the Mystical Way

forms. There are those who envision the divine as existing at a vast distance from the material world. The soul's ascent to union must literally transcend the chasm that separates the human from the divine, the secular from the sacred, the temporal from the eternal. The journey is upward and outward. These mystics emphasize the Transcendence of God. There are those who envision the divine reality as dwelling at the center of the soul and consequently at the heart of the material world. The soul descends into its own interior depths or discovers in creation this indwelling God. The journey is downward and toward the within. These mystics emphasize the Immanence of God.[28]

I call attention to this paradox for three reasons. (1) Both positions contain elements of truth about God as experienced by mystics and theologians and ordinary human beings. However, these positions are symbolic systems, a product of the mind created to convey a meaning which partially reveals but also leaves concealed aspects of the reality it attempts to explain. (2) By acknowledging these differences at the theoretical level, apparent contradictions at the practical level become understandable. Inspired by the notion of God's transcendence, a mystic, like the ascetic, will emphasize the practice of denying the senses. Inspired by God's immanence, a mystic, like the artist, might emphasize the purified employment of the senses. (3) Finally, the transcendent view has had a greater impact on the development of Western thought than has the immanence view. It leads to—more accurately, it is the product of—the split world view that separates matter from spirit, the secular from the sacred, and the feminine from the masculine. In comparing the positions implicit in Underhill and Johnston, it is safe to say that Johnston clearly recognizes the immanence of God and attempts to reconcile the split caused by the exclusively transcendent vision. Underhill, writing more than a half century earlier, addresses a world ensconced in dualities and consequently almost belabors the point of needed reconciliation. In my opinion, the immanence of God, his presence dwelling within all of creation, must be given its full significance, not only because it reflects one aspect of the divine reality, but because that aspect has been so badly neglected in Western thought.

Perhaps a final comment needs to be made. While Jung and Teilhard are men whose lives and works reflect their rootedness in Christianity, in my analysis comparing the evolution of the human element and the development of the human psyche, I have emphasized the psychological phenomenon of human growth. In comparing Underhill and Johnston I have incorporated more explicitly the consequences of the Christian tradition into the discussion. In describing the path of the mystic and the science of meditation, it is assumed that the Christian faith is the loving response to the God who is revealed in the historical person of Jesus and in the transforming power of his Spirit and whose atoning love for men and women is enacted personally and cosmically in the course of history. Informed by the insights offered by Underhill and Johnston, let us re-examine the initial conclusions and the tentative hypothesis about adult growth toward integration.

The Initial Conclusions and Hypothesis Revisited

Underhill's research of Christian mystical literature and Johnston's discussion of the science of meditation from the perspectives of both the Eastern and Western traditions tend to affirm each of the conclusions originally suggested. Let us examine each of them now illumined by the second comparative analysis.

1. Life is the process of spiritualization—matter is becoming spirit, the unconscious is becoming conscious. We can think of the initial "stuff" of our life as the "givens" we receive from the environment which is our socio-cultural world as well as our familial world, and from the environment which is our genetic inheritance—our bodies. In a sense, this is the matter from which we are formed. Initially all of this "stuff" is "taken for granted"; it is the "given" undifferentiated aspect of our life. As the child grows through young adulthood, decisions are made which affect the individual's present as "givens from the past." They too may be more or less conscious. The "stuff" or "matter" of one's life is transformed naturally as it becomes incorporated into the individual's consciousness. It becomes transformed graciously as that consciousness is touched by the healing power of the Holy Spirit.[35] These "givens"—"the stuff" we "take for granted"—are like the matter that both forms and imprisons the psyche, that aspect in the phenomenon of the human being from which growth toward

spiritualization takes place. Underhill and Johnston affirm the conclusion that growth moves in this predictable direction.

2. Underhill and Johnston affirm the power of polar tensions and the need to employ alternately the principle of opposites. Figure 7 illustrates several of the more significant apparent paradoxes which are reconciled in the experience of the mystic. These are further discussed in connection with the fifth and sixth conclusions below.

3. The path of the mystic moves through critical thresholds. The periods of pain follow the pattern of disintegration, detachment, and separation from the old life. The states of pleasure describe the more integrated organization around a new level of consciousness—a new way of perceiving reality. The periods of purgation loosen, ultimately liberate us, from the conscious and unconscious fetters that bind us— the "matter" which formed our lives. We discover and embrace as our own our parental scripts, our aggressiveness—seductive or manipulative; devouring or destructive—our fears, guilt, and rage. Purgation of the spirit loosens, ultimately liberates us from the controlling power of the conscious ego itself. Purgation exposes both the unconscious and the conscious realms of the healing power of the indwelling Spirit.

4. We can compare the map of the mystic to the journey taken during the "second half of life" which is illustrated in Figure 4. Jung suggested that "mid-life" occurred between thirty-five and forty-five during his time. Since longevity has increased with the passage of the centuries, we might expect that it occurred earlier during the Middle Ages and may well occur later in the future—especially if adolescent dependency is further prolonged through more specialized education. Whenever it actually occurs in the life of a specific individual, the successive pattern of surrendering and of discovering more profound levels of consciousness moves the individual toward greater integration.

5 and 6. The enlightened mystic bears a close resemblance to the individuated self, schematically illustrated in Figure 6, who is energized by the dynamism created by reconciled polar tension. The neglected realm associated with the feminine—feeling, imagination, unacknowledged areas of the unconscious—has been explored and exposed to the transforming power of the Spirit. The purgating but ne-

glected behavior of surrender and receptivity has been experienced and is embraced. The journey outward has been completed by a journey to the center and by an enlightened return to the activity of the market place.

These conclusions give further credence to the tentative hypothesis concerning a model for adult spiritual growth toward integration.

Adult human growth toward integration is
    a process of spiritualization
    which will proceed naturally if
    the neglected realm of interiority
    symbolically associated with the feminine
    is dialectically reconciled with
    the dominant realm of exteriority
    symbolically associated with the masculine.

Adult growth toward integration
    will proceed graciously if
    the process of spiritualization
    is touched by the transforming power
    of the Holy Spirit.

CHAPTER IV

MYTHIC SYMBOLS AND
THE DEVELOPMENT OF
CONSCIOUSNESS

The first part of my search for a model of adult spiritual growth is an effort in discovery—a search for patterns of relationship in the thought of two persons concerned with the phenomenon of human development. Teilhard and Jung have imaginatively envisioned the dynamics of growth and have created constructs—word labels—to deal with its development. Underhill and Johnston have explored the spiritual dimension of growth by researching mystical experience in Christianity and in the East. My search for relationships has been both dialectic and circular. The six tentative conclusions reflect my initial effort to synthesize diverse materials into a meaningful whole. These conclusions remained the focus to which I returned and into which I incorporated insights from Underhill and Johnston. My synthesis has been selective but basically uncritical.

I continue this spiraling approach through the remainder of my search, but with two deviations. The work of Erich Newmann is itself a search for symbolic patterns in the evolution of human consciousness—one which I appreciate but criticize for its incompleteness. The work of Robert Ornstein and others on bi-modal consciousness is itself predicated on laboratory data and supported by experiential evidence. Finally, I shall house my model in the context of Donald Gelpi's experience-based philosophical theory of the emergent self. The second part of my search for a model of adult spiritual growth is a brief venture in verification. It is an attempt to validate the model through dialogue with Neumann and mythic thought, with Ornstein and scientific thought, and with Gelpi and philosophical thought. The first part of my search tends to be intuitive and holistic; the second, rational and analytic.

The Origin and History of Consciousness

The evolution of consciousness
    in the life of humanity and
the development of ego consciousness
    in the life of the individual
    passes through a series of stages—
        archetypal patterns—
        which are organically related to each other and
        which are the main constituents of Western mythology.

This archetypal sequence is
    characteristic of cultures in which
ego consciousness has evolved creatively, that is,
    has absorbed more and more contents
        from the unconscious and
    has progressively extended its frontiers.

These archetypal patterns
    within the individual
    must be understood as "transpersonal," that is,
        internal structural elements in the psyche
        shared with all humanity.
    They are not simply personal elements
    in the life of the individual.
    These primordial images
    are contained in the collective unconscious.
    They become personalized as
    the conscious ego recognizes their influence
    within its psyche.[1]

Primordial images must be interpreted as symbols—
    psychic patterns expressed in varied modes.
This is especially important when
        the terms "masculine" and "feminine" are used.
            These terms are symbolic expressions;
                they do not describe sex-linked characteristics.
Sexual symbolism is transpersonal and archetypal;
        it is erroneous to project the characteristics of the symbol
            on persons of the symbol's sex.[2]
Unfortunately, our culture commits this error.

The sequential mythic stages
        in the evolution of consciousness and
        in the development of the ego
            include eight archetypal patterns—
            many of which have been alluded to
            in the preceding chapters—
The Uroborus
    The Great Mother
        The Separation of the World Parents
The Hero is born.
        The Hero slays the Terrible Mother.
        The Hero slays the Terrible Father.
The Hero captures the treasure.
        The Hero is transformed.

The Uroborus—
        the symbol of origination—
        appears as The Round Container—
        the Maternal Womb and
        the union of the World Parents.
            The masculine and feminine opposites
            are united in the Uroboric Round.

All that is deep
        pertains to this archetype—
            an abyss, the ground, the sea—
            the earth, the underworld, a cave.

It is the natural place—
    our original state of unconsciousness.
    It is the material from which we emerge;
    it is the maternal womb.[3]

The Uroboric Round—
    symbolized by the serpent consuming its tail—
    contains the universe—
    the World Parents in union
    the symbol of everlasting life
        the image of the creative impulse
        the initial upward spiral of evolution.[4]

The creative principle
    within the Great Round
    combines the notions of
        the initial movement of the paternal procreative thrust and
        the receptivity of the maternal procreative matter.

The Uroborus is consciousness' place of origin.
    The dawn of consciousness occurs
    as it becomes detached from
        the unconscious matter that encompasses it.
The ego emerges to confront the external world
    frightfully weak
    heavily dependent on the parents who bore it and
    fearful of being overwhelmed, consumed, devoured
        by that from which it has come.
Detachment from the Uroborus,
    entry into the world, and
    encounter with the principle of opposites
        are the essential tasks of human development.[5]

The Great Mother—
    the maternal element of the Uroborus—
    becomes, for the ego, potentially fatal.
    While once a place of contentment and
    remaining a source of nourishment,
        the maternal Uroborus turns to darkness and night.

The Great Mother now poses the ego
    with the threat of castration, death, and dismemberment.
    The Terrible Mother possesses the power
        to destroy consciousness as it
        struggles for autonomy and separateness.
    In its struggle
        the ego relies on a series of strategies—
        fear, flight, defiance, resistance.
Finally, the ego must slay the Terrible Mother
    to establish itself as separate from
    the overwhelming power of this transpersonal parent.[6]

The Separation of the World Parents is
    the first defiant act of human consciousness
        which splits off opposites from
        their original Uroboric unity.
    The Sky-Father is cast into the heavens—
        the light which rules the day from above.
    The Great Mother remains of the earth—
        the darkness, the void which envelops from below.

In the act of knowing
    consciousness achieves deliverance from the unconscious.
    This initial act of consciousness
    dismembers the Uroboric Round by
        splitting the First Parents—above and below,
    establishes the ego as separate, as other, as different, and
    sunders the world into opposites—
        into subjects and objects.

Subsequently, the conscious ego
    detaches itself from the realm of the body—
        the representative of the unconscious,
        the inner world of mood, emotion, and instinct; but
    suffers a sense of loneliness, or isolation.
The ego becomes conscious in a negative act—
    it says "no" to the Great Mother.

Consciousness continues
to discriminate, to distinguish, to mark off;
to isolate itself from its surrounding context.[7]

The youthful ego experiences its own weakness, and
its inadequacy to cope with the surrounding world;
it dreads its own separateness and
fears it will succumb to the seduction of the unconscious;
it suffers a sense of guilt at having severed the original unity.
The ego must become the Hero.

In the Hero Archetype
Neumann finds the constituent elements
in the evolution of human consciousness and
in the personal development of individual consciousness.[8]

In addition to the dark terrible side
of the Great Mother
which casts a threatening shadow over the newborn ego
there stands another side—
one which is bright, beautiful, and beneficent.
The Hero-Ego is born of the Great Mother;
it must extricate itself from the matrix
of her Terrible Aspects.
Later it will discover her beneficent aspects.

The Hero-Ego must leave the matriarchate—
the world of nature and matter, and
must enter the patriarchate—
the world of culture and spirit.

The Hero-Ego must be swallowed up
by the spirit of the culture;
must be educated into the patriarchy and
must be born-again into the higher realm
into the spiritual collective.

However, for the Hero-Ego to be consumed
　　by the collective cultural conscious
　　　　is to be imprisoned by the Terrible Father.[9]

The Hero-Ego
　　stands between the World Parents
　　　　each possessing a positive and a negative aspect.
The Hero-Ego must struggle against these opposing negative forces
　　and in the struggle achieve personal emancipation
　　from the tenacious grip of these Uroboric powers.[10]
The Hero fights a double dragon
　　to achieve the captive treasure.

The Terrible Mother is the first Dragon the Hero-Ego fights.
　　This dragon is the ego's inner darkness, its shadow;
　　the psyche's undeveloped parts which threaten
　　　　to engulf the ego in black confusion,
　　　　to overwhelm it with instinctual urges,
　　　　to expose its negative moods and emotions
　　　　once buried with bodily unconsciousness.

If the Ego-Hero
　　enters the chthonic realm,
　　penetrates this inner darkness, and
　　engages the Terrible Mother
　　　　without suffering its own destruction
then, the Hero-Ego emerges matured and
　　in possession of the Other Aspect of the Great Mother—
　　the beautiful, beneficent aspects of its own inner realm.

The Terrible Father is the second Dragon the Hero-Ego fights.[11]
　　The destructive, negative father is
　　　　the collective conscious of cultural convention
　　　　internalized in the rigid persona.
The Terrible Father imprisons the Hero-Ego in
　　the traditional norms
　　the paternal authority of the old order

the prevailing ideology—forces which seek
   to conserve the status quo and
   to prevent the conscious ego
   from its own constructive activity.[12]

The Terrible Father castrates consciousness
   in one of two ways—
   by captivating it in the cultural norms
   by making it dependent on paternal authority and
      thereby severing its creative power, or
   by identifying it with the cultural spirit
   by inflating it with detached arrogance
      thereby severing it from its earthly parts.
The ego is possessed by a rigid persona or
   it is inflated with heavenly *hybris.*[13]

The Hero-Ego which fails to slay
   the Terrible Mother remains
   a "mother's child"
      entombed in the womb—a victim of the unconscious
      cut off from the creative solar side of life.
The Hero-Ego which fails to slay
   the Terrible Father becomes
   a "father's child"
      incarcerated in a spiritual uterus—
      a victim of the cultural consciousness and
      cut off from the creative unconsciousness.[14]

The Hero who kills the Dragon claims the Treasure.
   When the Hero-Ego successfully slays the Terrible Aspects
   of the World Parents,
      it claims the captive-treasure
      held within the inner realm of the psyche.
With the Dragon's death
   the captive soul—the beautiful, beneficent aspects
   of the Great Mother
   is liberated to become

the counterpart of the ego
the complement of consciousness.

The active outwardly-oriented conscious ego
discovers its receptive part within its psyche and
enters into a friendly alliance with
the once alien world
of the body
of instinct
of the unconscious
the psychic elements
which have remained unacknowledged and undeveloped.[15]

The Dragon Fight—
the Ego's effort to resolve its conflict
with the transpersonal parents—
is repeated throughout life
in childhood, during adolescence, at mid-life—
whenever a rebirth or reorientation of consciousness occurs—
for the captive is the "new element" within the psyche
whose liberation makes further development possible.[16]

The Hero-Ego is Transformed in the process of centroversion.
Personality develops in three dimensions—
The first is an outward adaptation
to the world of things—the way of extraversion.
The second is an inward adaptation
to the world of symbols—the way of introversion.
The third is the self-forming, individuating tendency
which proceeds within the psyche itself—
the way of centroversion.[17]

The Hero-Ego is transformed
when consciousness faces inward
acknowledges its limitations becoming aware of The Self
around which the ego revolves.

The Ego assimilates contents from its unconscious and allows
the psyche's center to shift
from itself to The Self.

Before exploring the relevance of Neumann's use of mythology
to interpret the development of individual ego conscious to the psychological model of adult spiritual growth, I shall make four observa-
tions about Neumann's work itself. First, since the sequential pattern
of development concludes with the archetype of transformation, one
might assume that this stage of human consciousness has been realized. Certainly individuals have completed the entire mythic cycle of
the Hero. However, I suggest that our cultural consciousness has not.
For the most part, contemporary consciousness has yet to fight the
dragon. We have never engaged the Terrible Mother. Instead of entering the darkness of the inner realm, we deny its existence; we re-
press its instinctual impulses; we ignore the unconscious—its personal
repressed contents and its creative undeveloped contents. Moreover,
we have failed to free ourselves from the Terrible Father. Instead we
are imprisoned by the cultural norms; we are culturally identified
with a rigid persona; we are dominated by the patriarchy and cut off
from the collective unconscious. The contemporary social order is in-
carcerated in a patriarchal system.

Second, throughout his discussion, Neumann insists that "masculine" and "feminine" are symbolic terms, not literal expressions; that
"consciousness, as such, is masculine even in women, just as the unconscious is feminine in men."[18] However, it becomes increasingly
evident that the mythology of the Great Mother and of the Hero concerns the struggles of the male ego and not the conscious ego in gen-
eral. As a woman I can, on the one hand, identify with the basic
struggle of the conscious ego against the potentially devouring power
of the Terrible Mother. The darkness of the inner unknown and the
power of instinctual nature threaten women as well as men. On the
other hand, as a woman it becomes impossible to identify with the
genitally specific imagery of the phallic cult and the son-lover.

Neumann promises to resolve the problem of consciousness development in women when he deals with the psychology of the feminine. Unfortunately he died before completing an adequate
explanation of how consciousness develops differently in women. An

54

initial essay on "The Psychological Stages of Feminine Development" published in mimeographed form the year prior to his death is descriptive of generations of women whose life, according to the conventional norms of Western culture, culminated as the dependent partner in a patriarchal marriage.[19] Unfortunately, this description is accurate for many women, but is it normative for feminine development? I suggest that Neumann's feminine psychology is limited. It describes a convention of our culture; it is not constitutive of the development of consciousness in women. Quite simply, it fails to account for the increasing number of educated women who successfully contribute to industry, government, and the professions.

I agree with Donald Gelpi who argues that Neumann's use of mythic imagery describes, perhaps is constitutive of, the development of consciousness in men within male dominated societies.[20] I suggest that Neumann falls victim to the error he hoped to avoid. Masculine images especially in the Hero mythology of patriarchal societies have been interpreted literally rather than symbolically. The Hero-Ego has become sex-linked to male persons.

For women who might feel puzzled or left out of Neumann's interpretation of consciousness development and its gender-related imagery, I offer a possible resolution. I suggest that consciousness emerges from its opposite—the unconscious; that autonomous separateness is achieved in opposition to dependent union; that the body's spontaneous impulses differ from the mind's logically calculated conclusion; that light opposes darkness in women as well as in men. I suggest that for women, a polarity which places what-is-consciously-developed in the psyche at one pole and what-is-undeveloped-and-unconscious in the psyche at the other pole might be more useful than the gender-related polarity.

Third, I acknowledge that unfortunate historical fact that generations of women did not develop an autonomous conscious ego either by choice or through the conditioning of the patriarchal culture. As Donald Gelpi argues, "heroic imagery is profoundly sexist in character and consequently the hero myth which shapes our culture schools women to affective and intellectual passivity."[21] However, ample evidence suggests that women today, less limited by the rhythm of the reproductive cycle, will not be limited to the sexist cultural stereotype. Rather women, in increasing numbers, will not only realize higher levels of individual consciousness but will extend the frontiers of human consciousness.

Finally, I acknowledge that in the process of consciousness development sex-linked characteristics may well function to inhibit or to facilitate the growth of persons of one sex more than persons of the other sex. On the one hand, a young girl's sense of sex-identity does not demand that she see herself as "other" from her mother. This is not the case for the small boy. For him, his achievement of sex-identity facilitates his development of consciousness; for her it does not. On the other hand, men are not affected by the natural inner rhythm of the reproductive cycle and consequently have less occasion to listen to their inner world, to take account of their bodily reactions. Physiologically men may feel the need for physically aggressive behavior more frequently than women; women may feel the need for receptive behavior. However, I myself believe that these biological sex-linked characteristics are essentially independent of the development of consciousness.

Neumann and the Model of Adult Spiritual Growth

Neumann's exploration of the evolution of consciousness in the life of humanity and in the life of the individual illumines in new ways several conclusions concerning the developmental model of spiritual growth.

1. The archetypal stages, organically related and sequentially ordered, confirm the predictability of the growth pattern—a pattern which begins in the undifferentiated uroboric round, the unconscious, material place of origin. It moves in the direction of consciousness, of autonomy, of the spirit. However, the same uroboric symbolism that stands at the beginning of life, before the ego develops, reappears at the end of life when ego-development is replaced by the development of the Self. For the individuated Self, the principle of opposites no longer predominates and the uroboric round is replaced by the circular mandala. The goal of the second half of life is to incorporate the contents of the unconscious, to become independent of the world, and to stand by oneself.[22] The *alpha* and the *omega*—the place of origin and the goal of human wholeness—are appropriately symbolized by the circle. The path from the one to the other is not a straight line;

rather, the predictable path of human life itself can be symbolized as a circular motion.

The archetypes of the transpersonal parents provide insight into "the matter"—"the stuff" of our lives that becomes transformed into the human spirit. The Terrible Mother and the Terrible Father are the respective guardians of the internal unconscious and of the external collective conscious. Through the power of the shadow or of the persona each transpersonal parent can possess and imprison the ego. The process of spiritual transformation occurs when the ego engages each of these dragons and exposes the contents of the personal unconscious or of the rigid persona to the light of consciousness, ultimately to the healing power of the Holy Spirit.

2. Polar tension releases the psychic energy which propels human growth. The Dragon Fight and the captive's release provide an archetypal image for the energy generated through the opposition of polarity. The ego—the conscious developed part of the psyche—confronts the undeveloped and imprisoned parts of its psyche. The Treasure is the Captive, the new energy released by the ego's acceptance of the psyche's inner darkness, its repressed feelings, its bodily instincts. The Dragon Fight is repeated throughout life—in childhood, in adolescence, during mid-life. The conditions vary but it has occurred whenever a rebirth or reorientation of consciousness takes place, "for the captive *is* the new element whose liberation makes further development possible."[23]

3 and 4. The Dragon Fight symbolizes not only life's critical thresholds which the individual passes through in childhood, in adolescence and at mid-life but also the occasions of death-rebirth events that can be used toward spiritual growth. As the ego grows toward greater autonomy and conscious control of its life, it becomes detached from the rest of the psyche—detached from feelings, from bodily instincts. It becomes inflated with its own interests and importance, filled with what the Greeks called *hybris,* and finally commits the "inflated act." Deflated by its foolishness and failure, it experiences disorientation, disillusionment, and rejection.[24] When the ego is deflated, when its control over its world has disintegrated, the conditions are optimal for conversion and for renewal. The ego's controlling power has disintegrated, it becomes detached from its old ways. By confronting aspects of its shadow or rigid persona it becomes liber-

ated from the conscious or unconscious fetters that have bound it. This period of purgation is then followed by a period of renewal and of reintegration. This cycle of ego-inflation, purgation, and renewal can occur repeatedly during life. On a larger scale and in a more dramatic way it can occur at mid-life when the way of ego-development characteristic of the first half of life is replaced by the way of self-development characteristic of the second half of life. This cyclic pattern is experienced at its most profound level in the life of the mystics. Purgation of the spirit loosens and ultimately liberates the individual from the controlling power of the conscious ego itself.

5 and 6. I have argued above that while sexual symbolism is sometimes useful in identifying the polarity of opposites, its literal misuse contributes negatively to the self-understanding of women and reinforces sexist attitudes in men. The masculine imagery in the myth of The Hero is no exception. However, I suggest that the Hero Myth symbolizes the human story from the ego's perspective—one specific element in the human psyche. Perhaps another archetype would more adequately encompass the whole story of the human psyche. Neumann himself offers such a hint when he suggests that the Uroboric Round where the polar opposites reside in union is repeated in the circular mandala where the polar opposites are reconciled. These images encompass the beginning and the goal of the human story. They also suggest that the archetype of The Androgyne might more appropriately symbolize the whole human story—from beginning to end—from the perspective of human wholeness. Although it too can be misused, the archetype of the Androgyne incorporates through reconciliation the symbolic sexual polarities. My suggestion seems to be the implicit position of Barbara Charlesworth Gelpi whose essay "The Androgyne"[25] critiques Neumann's work and the explicit position of June Singer whose book *Androgyny*[26] explores the archetype of the androgyne through various cultural and historical contexts. The suggestion is also supported by James Hillman, who, in *The Myth of Analysis*[27] argues for a bisexuality of consciousness. However, prescinding from the sexist character of the Hero archetype, taken in its entirety, the Hero journey does deal with—albeit from the masculine perspective—the basic polarities in human life: independence and relatedness; solitude and involvement; consciousness and the unconscious; activity and receptivity.

CHAPTER V

TOWARD A COMPLETE
PSYCHOLOGY OF CONSCIOUSNESS

Neumann's thesis that individual ego development follows the archetypal patterns contained in the Hero myth provides insight into the powerfully held sexist attitudes prevalent in our patriarchal culture. It explains our devaluation of the inner realm of human life—the unconscious, the functions of feeling and intuition. It identifies the almost overwhelming cultural obstacles to an acceptance of a model for wholistic human growth.

Freud's understanding of the unconscious reinforces the sexist perspective of the hero archetype. For him the unconscious is the negative container of repressed feeling and instinct. It functions as a powerful threat to the conscious ego. Jung's understanding of the unconscious is more inclusive than Freud's. The unconscious is not merely a negative container of repression but is also a source of purpose and meaning for the individual. The unconscious contains the potential, undeveloped aspects of the psyche including The Self and it demonstrates mythic patterns or archetypes which seem to be shared among people in many cultures. Jung provides us with a positive interpretation of the unconscious—a symbolic system which values the inner realm and its significant contribution to wholistic human growth.

Robert Ornstein's effort to establish a complete psychology of consciousness provides us with another kind of positive evidence supportive of the ordinarily neglected inner realm. He and others have amassed laboratory data indicating that (1) we construct our "ordinary" consciousness, (2) the hemispheres of the brain perform specialized functions, and (3) the intuitive holistic mode of consciousness is the functional specialty of the right hemisphere.

We Construct Our Ordinary Consciousness

Our normal, waking, rational consciousness
    is one special type of consciousness.
    Parted from it by the filmiest of screens
        lie potential forms of consciousness entirely different.[1]

Our ordinary conscious
    is our linear, analytic, verbal mode of knowing.
    It is ego-centered.
    It has been the object
        of scientific inquiry and
        of mythological investigation.
The ordinary mode of knowing
    corresponds to the consciousness of the ego
    whose development
        in humanity and
        in the individual
        Erich Neumann traces through
        eight archetypal stages.
For Robert Ornstein
    our ordinary consciousness
    is a personal construction
    which we create
        in order to survive in the world.[2]

"Our normal consciousness is not
    a passive registration of our external environment.
    It is a highly evolved, selective, personal construction
        designed primarily for individual biological survival."[3]

Our ordinary consciousness is highly selective because
    our sense organs are selective in what they receive and
    our brains create "categories"
        which further limit our awareness
        of the external world "out there."

Each of our sense organs selects only
    certain aspects of the environment
    which is available to them.
    For example,
        of the entire electromagnetic spectrum
        the eye "sees" only a tiny band of radiation.

It is easy to assume that
    what we see, hear, touch or taste
        of the world "out there"
    exhausts the extent of that world.
We validate what we have taken in
    by verifying our conclusions with
        the conclusions of others.
    We receive con-sensual validation, that is,
        we achieve agreement with our sensory perception.
However, the others with whom we have agreed
    are similarly limited.
        What we share is our common limitations.[4]
It is easy to confuse
    our common agreements with external realities.

Our brains further limit
    what our sense receptors receive.
The brain creates "categories"
    which sort the data we receive.
    The "category" such as "straight," "aggressive," "feminine"
        becomes "what we expect"
        when we are stimulated by certain
        objects, events, or persons.

Jerome Bruner demonstrates that
    what we experience
    what we become aware of
        is the "category"
        evoked by a particular stimulus.[5]
The brain actively organizes
    what the sense organs receive.
    We become aware of the brain's output—
        its models and categories—
        rather than the external stimulus.[6]
Our normal consciousness does not merely register
    our external environment;
        it selectively constructs what it knows.

Our ordinary conscious is a personal construction
    designed primarily for biological survival.
    To survive biologically
        humanity has adopted
        a mode of active manipulation of the environment.
    Primitive humankind needed to separate itself
        from anything that would destroy it.
Survival assumes an analytic posture toward the world.
    It forces us to focus attention on external events.
    It needs to recognize the linearity—
        the sequence—between causes and effects.
    Language and science are sophisticated outcomes
        of the need to survive.
    "Their sequential structure allows us
    to dissect, discriminate, and divide
        the external environment into consistent segments
        that can be manipulated."[7]

Science is the refinement of our ordinary personal consciousness.
    It is one of
        the most restricted and
        the most sure forms of human knowledge.

Our culture is based on
>   this active-analytic-linear mode of consciousness—
>   the way of science, of language, and of history.

Our ordinary consciousness is designed
>   for the primary purpose of biological survival.
>   The sense organs and the brain
>   select aspects of the environment
>   most relevant for survival.
>   Ordinary consciousness is object-centered;
>   it involves analysis—
>   a separation of oneself from other objects.
Our ordinary consciousness enables us
>   to experience a relatively stable personal world.
>   The concepts of
>   causality, linear time, and language
>   are the essence of this mode.[8]
>   This mode of knowing, the mode of science,
>   is the dominant influence in our culture.

The Hemispheres of the Brain Perform Specialized Functions

Empirical and clinical research suggests that
>   the two hemispheres of the brain
>   perform specialized functions.
The left hemisphere
>   which governs the right side of the body
>   is adept at taking things apart and
>   at dealing with the separate parts
>   one at a time—
>   in a sequential process.
The right hemisphere
>   which governs the left side of the body
>   is good at grasping patterns of relations and
>   at integrating them into a whole
>   all at once—
>   in a simultaneous process.

The conscious mode of the left brain is
    analytical and sequential.
    It governs language
        which labels the separated parts.
    It is linear looking for
        the sequential, temporal, causal relationships
        among the parts.
    The left brain governs
        our ordinary mode of consciousness—
        the mode of ego-consciousness.

Evidence for the differences
    in hemispheric functions
    comes from several sources.
Victims of brain damage
    suffer different kinds of disabilities.
    If the left brain is injured
    language ability may be destroyed
        as in the case of aphasia
        and the patient is unable to speak.
    A similar injury to the right brain
    does not interfere with language but
        spatial awareness is severely disturbed and
        patients may be unable to dress themselves.[9]

The two hemispheres of the brain
    have been surgically separated
        for treatment of certain rare cases of epilepsy.
The Corpus Callosum—
    the bridge at the base of the brain
    which contains connecting nerve-fiber bundles—
    is severed
        rendering each hemisphere
        independent of the other.
    Amazingly, patients exhibit no apparent change
        in their overt behavior or
        in their personality.

However, when given specific tasks to perform
    requiring one of the specialized functions
        of the brain,
    noticeable differences occur.

To understand the nature of these specialized tasks
    it is necessary to recall that
    (1) language—speaking, listening, reading, writing—
    is mediated through the left brain.
        The disconnected right brain is unable
        to express itself verbally, and
    (2) the neural pathways which carry information
    from one side of the body and
    from one-half of the visual field
        cross over and connect only with
        the opposite side of the brain.
This means that the tactile data
    about an unseen object held in the left hand
    is communicated initially to
        the right hemisphere.
However, in split brain patients
    the Corpus Callosum no longer
        bridges the two hemispheres.
Thus, when asked questions about
    the unseen pencil held in the left hand
    the patient's mute, disconnected right brain
        is unable to respond verbally but
        can indicate its experience of the pencil
        by selecting a pencil from an array of objects.

Drs. Roger Sperry and Joseph Bogen
    have amassed dramatic evidence
    indicating the dissociation
        between the experiences of
        the two disconnected hemispheres of the brain.
Their data support the conclusion that
    the disconnected left brain—
        functioning in isolation from the right brain—

responds easily to verbal tasks but
cannot perform non-verbal, spatial tasks.
The left brain can verbally direct
    the right hand to draw a house;
it cannot visually direct
    the right hand to copy a drawing of a house.
The opposite is true for the right brain.
The disconnected right brain can visually direct
    the left hand to copy the drawing of a house—
    a spatial task;
it cannot direct the left hand to draw a house.[10]

In normal circumstances
    the Corpus Callosum connects
    the two hemispheres of the brain.
When such a person is asked
    to describe a hidden object held in the left hand,
    the tactile data are communicated first to the right brain and
        then across the Corpus Callosum to the left brain
        which provides a verbal description.
The Corpus Callosum bridges
    the two hemispheres
    rendering possible
        the functional specialty—
        the mode of consciousness—
        appropriate to the situation.
When connected,
    how do the two hemispheres relate to each other?

On the one hand
    it would seem that
    the two modes of consciousness
        are complementary—
    the analytic mode provides
        what the holistic mode lacks
        and vice versa.
Reports of artists and scientists
    reflecting on their own creativity
        support the notion of a complementary relationship.

They suggest that
    (1) they have developed both modes of consciousness
        the rational-analytic and
        the intuitive holistic,
    (2) they have learned to inhibit
        one or the other
        when its mode is inappropriate, and
    (3) they have used both modes in
        an alternating complementary fashion.

On the other hand
    it would seem that
    the two modes of consciousness
        may conflict with each other.
For example,
    the left brain's need to note detail
        in a form suitable for expression in words
    may interfere with
        an over-all perception of the whole, or
    the right brain might interfere with
        efforts to reconcile a checking account.[11]

On a more profound level
    conflict between hemispheric specialization
        seems to resemble
    conflict between the conscious and unconscious processes
    as psychoanalytic theory understands it—that is
        the conflict between
        the conscious ego and
        the repressed contents of the personal unconscious.
Clinical evidence shows that
    split brain patients
    who receive disturbing, emotion-laden information
        in their right brain and are
        unable to process it verbally,
    behave in an apparently "defensive" manner
        remarkably similar to
        the psychoanalytic processes of
        repression and denial.

Ornstein succinctly describes
    the response of one of Roger Sperry's patients.

> In the course of a series of otherwise dull laboratory tests, a
> photograph of a nude woman was shown to the right
> hemisphere of a patient. At first, the woman viewing the
> pinup on the screen said that she saw nothing, then
> immediately flushed, alternately squirmed, smiled, and
> looked uncomfortable and confused. But her "conscious" or
> verbal side was *still* unaware of what had caused the
> emotional turmoil. All that was accessible to the verbal
> apparatus was that *something* unusual was occurring in her
> body. Her words reflected that the emotional reaction had
> been "unconscious," unavailable to her language
> apparatus.[12]

Commenting on the same research, Galin observes that

> there seems to be a parallel between the functioning of the
> isolated right hemisphere and mental processes which are
> repressed, unconscious, and unable directly to control
> behavior. These similarities suggest the hypothesis that in
> normal, intact people mental events in the right
> hemisphere can become disconnected functionally from the
> left hemisphere (by inhibition of neuronal transmission
> across the Corpus Callosum) and can continue a life of their
> own. This hypothesis offers a neurophysiological mechanism
> for at least some instances of repression, and an anatomical
> locus for the unconscious mental contents.[13]

The phenomenon of an isolated right brain
    may occur in persons
    whose hemispheres remain intact.
The individual may actively inhibit
    the transfer of information
        from one hemisphere to the other
        due to the negative or conflicting nature of the data.

For example,
       a mother may present her small child
              with one message verbally but
       communicate another message
              with her facial expression and body language.
       Her words say "I do this because I love you."
       Her face says "I hate you and will destroy you."
              The child's left brain processes the words;
              the right brain experiences the facial gestalt.
Different, conflicting messages
       have been delivered—one to each hemisphere;
       opposite responses are called for—
              the left brain wants to "approach";
              the right brain wants "flight."
The child is caught in the familiar dilemma.
In situations demanding overt activity
       the left brain tends to predominate;
       the child needs the nurturance of the mother
              and follows the lead of the left brain.
Although it can weaken the access between hemispheres,
       the left brain cannot just
       "turn off" the right brain's experiences.
       The contents of the right brain—
              the face and body language which said
              "I hate you and will destroy you"—
       may continue a life of its own
              independent of rational processing.[14]

Clinical evidence suggests that
       the human brain is capable of two modes of consciousness.
       The rational-analytic mode
       for nearly all right-handed persons—
              about 95% of the population—and
       for some left-handed persons
              appears to be housed in the left hemisphere of the brain.
       The intuitive-holistic mode of consciousness
              appears to be the functional speciality
              of the right hemisphere.

69

The rational-analytic mode of the left hemisphere
     appears to be our "ordinary" consciousness
          concerned with events and objects in the external world.
     It is the consciousness of the ego—
          the consciousness of which Western civilization
          is most aware.
The functional speciality of the right hemisphere
     is far less familiar to us
     having been associated with the special giftedness
          of the artist, the creative scientist, and mystic; or
     relegated to the misfortunes
          of the pathological or the primitive.

The evidence suggests that
     the special functions of the hemispheres
     can relate to each other in at least two distinct ways.
          They may relate in a complementary manner; or
          they may relate in a contradictory, conflicting manner.

The Intuitive-Holistic Mode of Consciousness: What Can Be Said About It?

It is somewhat difficult to describe
     the functional speciality of the right hemisphere
          for two reasons.
     First, it is much more alien to our experience
          than our ordinary consciousness.
          We are less familiar with it and its workings.
     Second, language, my medium for expression,
          is a function of the rational-analytic mode.

I shall attempt to describe the intuitive-holistic mode
     by creating a structure
          based on the more familiar rational-analytic mode
     and shall proceed
     in a sequential manner (!)
          to contrast it
          with the hope that

a descriptive gestalt of the intuitive-holistic mode
will emerge in the end!
The interface of these modes does create a challenge!

Whereas ordinary consciousness
is concerned with the external world,
with objects and events,
the "other" mode of consciousness
is concerned with the world within the individual—
with bodily awareness and movement,
with feeling and physical abilities,
with affectivity and imagination.
It tends to
the sensuous
the hidden
esoteric
non-verbal areas of experience.

Whereas the rational analytic mode of consciousness
mediates meaning sequentially,
is concerned with duration
with parts and their temporal relationship,
the intuitive-holistic mode of consciousness
seeks the meaningful whole
in an immediate, simultaneous process.
It tends to focus on
the gestalt
the patterned relationships
experienced in the present in a spatial way.
It is synthetic—
putting pieces together
searching for connections
suggesting similarities.
Whereas ordinary conscious is focused
the other mode is more diffuse.

Whereas the left brain functions
in an active mode and
proceeds in a logical verbal manner

the right brain functions
    in a receptive mode
    relying on
        awareness
        inspiration
        happy hunches and lucky guesses.
It uses intuition
    to imaginatively bridge data gaps;
it employs symbols
    to mediate meaning.

Whereas our ordinary consciousness of the ego
    has been symbolically associated with
        the light
        the masculine
        the Yang,
the other mode of consciousness
    similar to some of the processes of the unconscious
    has been symbolically associated with
        the dark
        the feminine
        the Yin.

Although the symbolic, intuitive mode of consciousness
    is less familiar to us
        than the functional speciality of the left brain
    we do encounter the functional speciality of the right brain
    in ordinary life but frequently
    we have failed to recognize its value.

Philosophers and learning theorists
    concerned with the nature of human knowledge and
    how it is acquired
        have identified the place of the symbolic, intuitive mode.
Jean Piaget describes symbolic thought
    as characteristic in the development of children
    the stage between sensory-motor consciousness of the infant

and the concrete operational thought
of the young school age child.
Unfortunately, he labels it as "autistic"
implying that it is only characteristic
of a primitive stage of development or
of a pathological state of the personality.[15]

Jerome Bruner, an advocate of the intuitive mode,
is concerned that students develop
an attitude toward learning which includes
guessing and postulating hunches—
a process similar to Piaget's
pre-operational child—
but he acknowledges that
the intuitive mode of consciousness
is associated with the
left hand—
awkward
suspect
sentiment, only art![16]

Donald Gelpi uses insights from Charles Pierce and Michael Polyani
to argue that rational inquiry
is preceded by "mind-play" and
is motivated by "heuristic passion."
Pierce's notion of abductive inference
bridges the realms of
the appreciative consciousness—
affectivity and imagination—and
the rational consciousness—
the inferential logic of deduction and induction.[17]

Psychologies concerned with human wholeness—
gestalt therapy, psychosynthesis, analytic psychology—
employ strategies that
facilitate the emergence of right brain consciousness.
Jung's understanding of the symbolic nature of dream material
is an outstanding example of the method of symbol.

Jung's theory of personality types
>makes assumptions consistent with
>>the right brain—left brain research.
The extraverted orientation compares with
>the external, object orientation
>of the left brain, while
the introverted orientation compares with
>the inner concerns
>of the right brain.
Each of the four functions—
>sensing and intuition
>>the two ways individuals prefer
>>to receive information into consciousness, and
>thinking and feeling
>>the two ways individuals prefer
>>to make decisions about the information received—
>can be easily associated with
>a hemispheric function.
The left hemisphere tends to operate primarily on
>perception through the senses and on
>judgments based on the logic of reason—
>>the sensing and thinking functions.
The right hemisphere tends to rely primarily on
>perceptions through intuitive insight and on
>judgments based on consistency with
>>an internalized set of values—
>>the intuitive and feeling functions.
The external world is the primary focus
>of individuals with an extraverted orientation and
>>who have developed the functions of
>>sensing and thinking.
The internal world is the primary focus
>of individuals with an introverted orientation and
>>who have developed the functions of
>>intuition and feeling.[18]

Persons concerned with understanding
  the processes of human creativity
    have investigated the realm of the right brain.
Galin's discussion of the complementarity
  of the two modes of consciousness as
    they function within the lives of
    artists and creative scientists
  is one among many instances of this point.[19]

Individuals seeking to understand religious experience
  seeking enlightenment within the Eastern traditions
  seeking union with God within the Christian tradition
predicate their searches
  on the implicit belief that
    other than the "ordinary" mode of consciousness
    is possible and is desirable.
The ascetical practices and
  the prayer-meditation techniques
  of the mystics in both the West and the East seek
    to disconnect our ordinary consciousness
    to surrender the ego's conscious control.
This allows
  the inner human spirit
  the transcendent Other
    housed at the core of the human heart
  the Divine Spirit
    to envelop our "other" consciousness—
"a potential form of consciousness
  parted from ordinary consciousness
  by the filmiest of screens."[20]

Recent clinical research into the functional specialties of the two hemispheres of the brain and its implications for the psychology of consciousness sheds new insights on two pairs of our six conclusions—the third and fourth which concern the critical thresholds or periods of transitions from an abandoned former mode of doing things to new ways of consciously organizing one's life; and the fifth and sixth conclusions which deal with the principle of opposites and their reconciliation.

Critical Thresholds Revisited: Conclusions 3 and 4

We have discussed critical thresholds in terms of the natural periods of transition between what developmental theories of growth call stages. We have also looked at critical thresholds in terms of ego-inflation as it occurs in small ways frequently during life and as it occurs in a big way for some persons at mid-life. We have compared both of these processes with the periods of purgation reported by the mystics. Study of the hemispheric specialities of the human brain suggests that learning to disconnect the conscious control of the left brain—at least temporarily—and allowing the right brain to function can create the conditions for creative growth. Such an event might be experienced as painful if, for example, non-processed negative experiences such as those contained in the personal unconscious were exposed to the rational left brain. Such an event might be experienced as joyful—the "ah ha" experience of intuitive insight. Such an event might be experienced as peaceful or painful—a consequence of periods of contemplative prayer. In any event, I suggest that if we construct our ordinary mode of consciousness, it is also possible to educate our other mode of consciousness—the specialized function of the right brain. We need not only await those moments in the course of life when external events or profoundly disturbing inner stages precipitate us into a crisis, but rather, we can create the conditions as a part of ordinary life that facilitate the emergence of our intuitive mode of consciousness—the one attuned to the inner realm of our ordinary life.

Bi-modal Consciousness and the Principle of Opposites: Conclusions 5 and 6

Clinical and empirical research on the specialized functions of the brain's hemispheres provides a physiological foundation for certain aspects of the principle of opposites and their reconciliation. It seems evident that the left brain's ego consciousness dominates patriarchal cultures and that in such cultures the right brain's intuitive mode is neglected and devalued. If we take seriously the fact that we construct our ordinary consciousness, that we construct "categories" in our consciousness to which we respond rather than respond directly to the impacting stimuli, we can better understand the sexist attitudes related to the literal, rather than the symbolic, use of the terms masculine and feminine to describe polar opposites. In the ordinary consciousness of our prevailing culture, the categories "masculine" and "rational-analytic" have become interchangeable; similarly, the categories "feminine" and "intuitive-holistic." I suggest that the method of science may have provided us with a more adequate explanation of differences in conscious modalities. The specialized functions of the hemispheres of the brain offer a physiological source of polar differences that is more encompassing—certainly less devastating to woman—than the traditional dichotomies between mind and body, mental and physical awareness; reason versus passion, mind versus intuition; we might begin thinking in terms of the bi-modal consciousness available to human life through the specialized function of the brain's hemispheres. Before we can begin to educate this neglected mode of consciousness we must surrender some strongly imbedded and widely cherished attitudes concerning the exclusive value of the rational-analytic ego-consciousness. The awareness of such a possibility—within an individual or within any segment of our culture—is tantamount to "a critical threshold" which, if crossed, is certain to bring both pain and new life.

The Six Conclusions: A Recapitulation

Conclusion One:

The evolution of the human psyche moves in a predictable direction—from the undifferentiated material world of the infant toward the spiritual world of the adult. Matter becomes spirit; the unconscious becomes conscious.

—Teilhard and Jung

Life is the process of spiritualization. The initial "stuff" of our lives are the "givens" we receive from our environments—the environment which is our social-cultural-familial world; the environment which is

77

our genetic inheritance—our physiological world. In the process of spiritualization the "stuff"—the givens from the past—is transformed naturally as it becomes incorporated into the individual's consciousness. It becomes transformed graciously as that consciousness is touched by the healing power of the Holy Spirit.

—Underhill, Johnston, and Gelpi

The archetypes of the Terrible Mother and The Terrible Father provide insight into the kinds of "matter"—the "stuff" of our lives in need of transformation into the individual's inner spirit and of healing by the power of the Holy Spirit. The uroboric round, symbolic of that place where human life originates, and the circular mandala, symbolic of human wholeness, the goal of human life, suggests that the predictable direction of human growth is circular—one which moves from a place wherein resides the union of opposites, through a period where polar opposition generates psychic energy, to an integrated state where polarities are reunited through reconciliation.

—Neumann

Conclusion Two:

The human psyche is propelled to grow through energy generated by tension created by polar opposites—tension created by extraverted activity directed toward the external world and by introverted activity directed toward the internal world in the psyche—tension between the conscious life of the psyche and its unconscious life.

—Teilhard and Jung

The Mystical Way suggests additional polarities that become reconciled. Periods of purgation—of pain, darkness, separation, destruction and death—alternate with states of pleasure—of light, union, construction, and life. Ultimately the non-attachment of the independent individual is reconciled in a uniting relationship with the interdependent many-union differentiates.

—Underhill and Johnston

The archetype of the Dragon Fight which liberates the Captive-Treasure suggests that the energy released when the conscious developed

78

part of the psyche confronts the undeveloped part—an imprisoned part is liberated and the new element or energy makes further development possible.

—Neumann

Conclusion Three:

Human growth occurs as the individual crosses a three-part critical threshold: (1) a period of disintegration, a separation from the former ways, (2) a period of painful transition and awkward behavior, and (3) a period of integration around a new way of organizing one's life. This "conversion" like experience is characteristic of the transition between stages described in developmental theories.

—Teilhard and Jung

The path of the mystic also moves through critical thresholds—periods of purgation followed by periods of pleasure and joy. The periods of purgation loosen, ultimately liberating the individual from the conscious and unconscious fetters that bind him or her. Purgation exposes the unconscious realm to the light of consciousness; it exposes the unconscious and the conscious realms to the healing power of the indwelling spirit.

—Underhill, Johnston and Gelpi

The Dragon Fight mythically expresses two major critical thresholds the individual ego must cross—separation from the parental scripts, the controlling influence of The Terrible Mother and The Terrible Father. As a culture we have never slain the Terrible Father and consequently remain in the destructive clutches of patriarchal attitudes and values. The individual ego must confront the contents of the shadow and of the rigid persona in a painful act of acceptance and of separation. The inflated ego, filled with what the Greeks called hybris, may commit numerous "inflated acts" during the course of its development; its mid-life crisis can be considered the big experience of ego-deflation, one which is followed by the emergence of the Self.

—Neumann, Jung, and Gelpi

The realization that the hemispheres of the brain perform two specialized functions and the fact that we construct our ordinary consciousness suggest that we can educate our right brain's intuitive-holistic mode of consciousness and that we can learn to inhibit the domination of the left hemisphere's mode of operation when it is inappropriate. An individual concerned about facilitating human growth and enriching the quality of human experience can create conditions as a part of ordinary life that encourage the emergence of the intuitive mode of consciousness.

—Ornstein and Galin

Conclusion Four:

In the course of human life, the individual can expect to confront a series of critical thresholds, or death-rebirth experiences. Analytic psychology identifies four critical moments—birth, adolescent-young adult independence, the mid-life crisis, and death. Other stage theorists have identified a different set of significant transitions.

—Jung

The Christian mystic way normally begins to appear in adults with mature egos at mid-life with a crisis or similar event of awareness that initiates the second half of life. That moment occurs when the ego ceases to demand its exclusive control over the activities of life, begins to acknowledge its own limitations, and gradually allows the power of the Immanent-Transcendent Other to direct its life.

—Underhill and Johnston

Conclusion Five:

Active, rational behavior has been associated symbolically with the masculine realm in contrast to its polar opposite—receptive, intuitive behavior, symbolically associated with the feminine. Similarly, consciousness is symbolized by the masculine; the unconscious, by the feminine. Contrasexual symbolism has been the traditional means of expressing the tension between the polarity of opposites.

—Jung

The enlightened mystic bears a close resemblance to the individuated self who is energized by the dynamism created by reconciled polarities. Activity in the market place alternates with receptive surrender to the power of the Spirit. Extraverted behavior is complemented by introverted behavior. Solitude of the independent individual is balanced by relatedness and a recognition of the interdependence of all humanity.

—Underhill and Johnston

The hemispheres of the brain with their specialized functions offer an alternative explanation for understanding polarity within the psyche—one which is more adequate and inclusive than the traditional symbols of the contrasexual principles. It is one which could eliminate much confusion and self-doubt among women, especially those who reject the cultural stereotype for feminine behavior. The realization that we construct our ordinary consciousness lends credence to the hope that, if motivated, we can educate the right brain's mode of intuitive consciousness.

—Ornstein and Galin

Conclusion Six:

The individuated self—the goal of human wholeness—enjoys the psychic situation where the polar opposites are reconciled with each other. Personal human concerns are united with universal human concerns. The unconscious mediates meaning to the conscious ego; introverted and extraverted activity alternate.

—Teilhard and Jung

The enlightened mystic and the individuated self complement the journey outward with a journey to the center and by an enlightened or reconciled return to the activity of the market place.

—Underhill and Johnston

While the Hero archetype may be appropriate to associate with the development of the conscious ego, it does not adequately encompass the development of the whole psyche—the development of the ego and the emergence of the self. The life cycle, symbolically placed between the uroboric round and the circular mandala—both symbols of united opposites—suggests that the archetype of the Androgyne might supplement, perhaps replace the archetype of the Hero, as the pattern for the whole of human development and for wholeness in human life.

—Neumann, Singer, B. Gelpi

The two hemispheres of the brain, each with its specialized function, suggest that within each individual—men and women—there is a physiological foundation for the development of a bi-modal consciousness—a consciousness capable of reconciling, when appropriate, the realms and modes of behavior, traditionally associated with contrasexual symbolism. All human persons possess the cerebral organ which, if developed, makes possible a reconciliation between the consciousness of the rational analytic left brain and the intuitive-holistic consciousness of the right brain.

—Ornstein and Galin

CHAPTER VI

THE EMERGENT SELF:
A PHILOSOPHICAL FRAMEWORK

The major philosophical traditions of the West
    have reinforced the split between
        the rational consciousness of spirit and
        the unconscious material of matter.

Neo-Platonic thought divides reality between
    spirit and matter
    the eternal and the temporal
    the sacred and the profane.

The Aristotelian tradition unifies reality into *essences*
    but divides essences into substance and accidents and
        substances into form and matter.
The essence of things can be conceived of in two dimensions
    substantial elements
        which constitute the nature of a being, and
    accidental elements
        which contribute the particular characteristics of
        individual substances.
Like all substances, human nature is conceived of
    in two dimensions—form and matter.
        The human spirit gives *form* to
        the *matter* of the human body.

The human spirit itself consists of
  two spiritual faculties
    the intellect and the will.

Although the Aristotelian tradition
    attempts to understand the unity of being
    it perpetuates the major divisions of Neo-Platonic thought and
    it places the separated parts into
      a superior-inferior relationship—
      substance over accidents
      spirit over matter
      mind over body.
The Aristotelian tradition has significantly influenced
    the pattern of language and of thought in the West.

The implications of science and technology
    have forced philosophers to rethink
      their basic assumptions about reality.
More recently philosophic thought has shifted from
    a concern for the substance of things to
    a concern for how things function.

Whiteheadian thought grounds reality in
    the process of experience.
    It is within this conceptual framework
    of process philosophy that
      Donald Gelpi has developed
      a theory of emergence in which
    experience, rather than essence,
      is the central unifying category in
      his model of the emergent self.

In a creative effort
    Gelpi has synthesized
    major portions of Whiteheadian thought with
    elements from other philosophers
      in the American tradition—
      notably Charles Peirce.

At the risk of over-simplification
    I shall attempt
        a non-philosophical description of
        Gelpi's theory of the emergent self.

Human experience is basically an interactive process
    between the individual and the environment.
    Put simply—
        The individual's environment
        exerts an impact on the individual and
        the individual responds
        to the environmental impact.

The "environment" can be conceived of in two ways—
    (1) our ordinary conception of environment
    which consists of our external world or
        our "sustaining environment" and
    (2) our internal environment—
    which consists of
    our physical bodies and the feelings and instincts they house
        our internal world which we sustain—
        our "sustained environment."
The impact on the individual may originate
    from either environment—
        it may be an impulse from within us or
        it may be an event from outside us.

The individual is conceived of as
    an "emerging self"
    an entity which maintains self-continuity
        through the habitual patterns it develops
        from past experiences—
    "habitual tendencies" which give direction
        to the self as it
        interacts in each present experience and
        emerges toward future experiences.

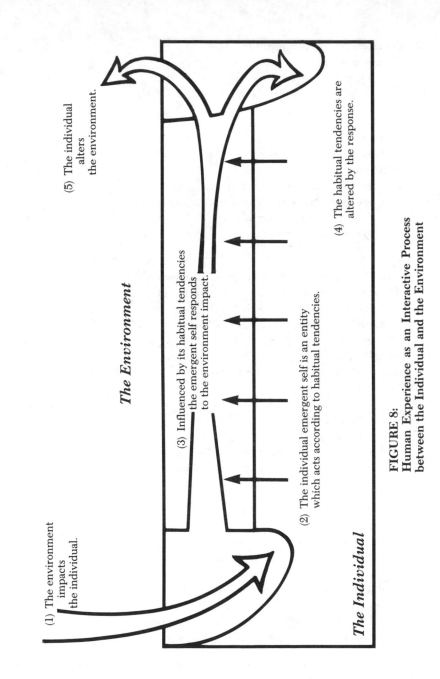

FIGURE 8:
Human Experience as an Interactive Process
between the Individual and the Environment

The reaction of the individual
　　can be conceived of in two ways
　　(1) as the self's evaluative response to the impact, and
　　(2) as the ultimate reaction to the impact as it affects
　　　　the emerging self and the environment.

The interactive process of human experience can be
　　schematically illustrated as
　　　　depicted in Figure 8 and
　　　　described in five phases.
　　(1) The environment impacts on the individual.
　　(2) The individual emergent self is an entity with
　　　　habitual tendencies to behave in a characteristic way.
　　(3) The emergent self uses its habitual tendencies
　　　　to respond to the environmental impact.
　　(4) When the response terminates, the habitual
　　　　tendencies of the emergent self are altered.
　　(5) When the response terminates, the environment
　　　　is ultimately altered.

The initial impact of a "fact"
　　impinging upon the senses
　　　　is never a simple registration
　　　　of an "objective" stimuli.
It is received into awareness
　　through a neural system
　　　　conditioned by previous emotional and perceptual images.

What we initially experience
　　has already been influenced to some extent
　　　　by the emergent self's habitual tendencies.
The individual may remain unaware of
　　this emotional conditioning;
　　　　the individual's response may terminate immediately
　　　　　　as in a reflex action.
The evaluative response to infants
　　is limited to this type of brief
　　　　and immediate reaction to sense perception.

As the individual is capable of a more sustained response
    these felt tendencies may disclose themselves
        more or less vaguely to the individual's consciousness.
    Gelpi has labeled these affective disclosures
        as the emergent self's "physical purposes."
"Physical purposes" encompass
    the individual's affective process and
        the processes of the imagination.

Feeling and imagination are closely connected.
    Feelings may be experienced
    as negative or as sympathetic;
        negative feelings may be repressed and
        remain unacknowledged by the individual.
Images may be of a personal or of a collective nature.
    They may be associated with the individual's life;
    they may share in the archetypal patterns
        found in many persons in many cultures.

When these physical purposes
    disclose themselves
        more consistently and more vividly,
    the individual develops an appreciative consciousness—
    a conscious awareness of
        the several levels of affectivity and
        the several kinds of imagery.[2]
In our culture we have failed to cultivate
    the appreciative consciousness.

Imagination with its intuitive insights
    renders possible the first type of inferential thought—
    that dimension of cognitive thought which responds by
        wondering if "such and such is the case"—by
        formulating a hypothesis.
Gelpi calls this type of inference "abduction"
    based on Charles Peirce's suggestion that
    there are three forms of inference—

abduction which tries to classify a factual impact,
deduction which attempts to clarify its meaning, and
induction which seeks to verify its truth.
Inferential thought is possible only in mature individuals
whose habitual cognitive tendencies are sufficiently developed
to significantly influence the emergent self's
evaluative response.[3]

One instance of human experience is concluded
as the individual terminates its evaluative response
with a "decision"—
one which reshapes the habitual tendencies
within the emergent self,
one which alters
the environment.

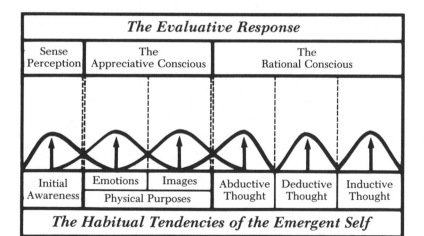

FIGURE 9:
The Array of Habitual Tendencies Whose Disclosure to Consciousness Differentiates the Evaluative Response of the Emergent Self within an Instance of Human Experience.

The array of habitual tendencies
    which significantly influence
    the quality of the emergent self's evaluative response
        is schematically illustrated in Figure 9.
The patterned arrangement of these tendencies
    characteristic of one instance of human experience
    is also characteristic of
    the development of differentiated responses
        in the course of life.
The infant is capable only of a sensory response;
    the young child may respond
        out of feeling or
        out of symbolic thought
    but is incapable of inferential thought;
        the mature adult is capable of differentiated inference.

The quality of human experience—
    the degree to which the evaluative response is differentiated—
    depends upon the degree to which the habitual tendencies
        are consciously developed and disclose themselves
            to the emergent self's awareness.

Gelpi's Theory of Emergence
    is valuable for many reasons;
    I explore only those relevant to my search.
"Experience" assumes that reality is not static
    but is a state of continuous change.
"Experience" is especially useful
    in a consideration of human growth.

Gelpi's model of the emergent self
    allows us to look at the experience of growth
        as the pattern of a lifetime or
        as the pattern of a single instance of life.

The conscious autonomous behavior of the mature adult
    emerges as a result of a developmental process

which began as the undifferentiated
sensory-motor reflex-reaction behavior of the infant
and achieves greater differentiation as
affective, cognitive, and moral development
each proceeds through its ordered pattern of growth.

A single instance of conscious autonomous behavior
emerges through the same sequence—
the sensory impact is followed by an affective response
then by a cognitive response and finally by a decision.

The model allows us to relate stage theories
concerned with affective, cognitive, and moral development.
The model also allows us to deal with depth psychologies
and the assumptions they make about human experience.
The construct of "the sustained environment"—
our inner world—
allows us to distinguish the kinds of impulses
that might impact the individual according to
psychoanalytic theory of the unconscious or
analytical psychology's notion of the unconscious.

The model allows us to see the place of
the two modes of consciousness and
creativity in the emergence of experience.

Figure 10 illustrates six applications
of Gelpi's theory.
These include (1) the pattern of an emerging experience
graphically presented at the top of the page
from left to right
from sense-perception to action-decision.
The remaining five applications are
graphically presented below but
in relation to the initial pattern.

1. The Emergence of Experience as the Pattern of a Lifetime and as the Pattern of a Single Instance

The Evaluative Response of the Emergent Self				
Sense Perception	The Appreciative Conscious	The Rational Conscious		Action Decision
	Physical Purposes	Inferential Thought		
	Emotions | Images	Abduction | Deduction | Induction		

2. The . . . The Neglected Realm . . . Dominant Realm

Sensing ⟷   Intuition ⟷   Sensing ⟷

3.   Feeling ⟷   Thinking ⟷

Jung's Four Functions

. . . Our Other Consciousness   . . . Our Normal Waking Ordinary Consciousness

4. . . . The Functional Specialty of the Right Brain   . . . The Functional Specialty of the Left Brain

. . . The Receptive Holistic Spatial Mode of Consciousness   . . . The Active Analytic Linear Mode of Consciousness

Ornstein's Hemispheric Functions

5.   Creativity ⟷

Combinatory Play
Mind Play
Heuristic Passions

Einstein
Pierce
Polanyi

6.   Happy Hunches   *Bruner*

Sensory-Motor Thought   The Representational Symbolic Thought of the Pre-operational Child.   The Concrete and Formal Operational Thought of the Older Person

Piaget's Stages of Cognitive Development

FIGURE 10:
Some Relationships between Gelpi's Model of the Emergent Self and Modes of Consciousness.

For example, (2) the neglected interior realm includes
  the disclosures of the physical purposes
    to the appreciative conscious and
  the initial hunches of abductive thought.

Jung's four functions (3)—
  sensing and intuition
  thinking and feeling—
    are located at the appropriate segments
    of the evaluative response.
  Feeling and intuition
    fall within the neglected realm.

Ornstein's hemispheric functions (4)
  can be easily placed in this theoretical context.

Similarly comments made about "creativity" (5)
  by notably creative individuals
  bridge the appreciative conscious and
    the rational conscious.

Finally, one developmental theorist—Piaget (6)—is represented.
  Piaget's stages of cognitive development
    are sequentially located
    across the model of an emergent experience.

Gelpi's Theory of the Emergent Self
  interprets the hypothesis that
  adult human growth toward integration
  will proceed naturally if the neglected realm
    of interiority
    of the appreciative conscious
    of the brain's right hemisphere
  is acknowledged
  is valued
  is developed
    and
  is dialectically reconciled

with the dominant realm
of exteriority
of the rational conscious
of the brain's left hemisphere.

Gelpi's basic faith assumption
which underlies his entire foundational theology
supports the hypothesis that
adult human growth toward integration
proceeds graciously
when both modes of consciousness
are touched by the transforming powers
of the Holy Spirit.

CHAPTER VII

SOME CONCLUDING IMPLICATIONS

The psychological model for spiritual growth suggests some concluding implications in several areas of human concern: prayer, spirituality, and social ministry; conversion, liminality, and stages of development; sexism, women's development, and wholistic human growth; and learning theory, modes of inquiry, and educational practice.

Prayer, Spirituality and Social Ministry

Some have suggested that spirituality and social ministry are opposing concerns in the Christian life; others suggest that spirituality and ministry are opposite sides of the same coin. Some have suggested that spirituality concerns only an individual's prayer life; others argue that their prayer is in their ministry.

One implication of the model suggests with Jung that there are two realms in human life—one which focuses outward, one which focuses inward. Some persons are more extraverted-oriented and find meaning in persons and events as external to themselves. They have developed gifts that deal with the exterior world. Other persons are more introverted-oriented and find meaning in the internal experience of persons and events. These have developed skills to deal with life from within their interior experience. While the gifts of both kinds of persons must be acknowledged and valued, neither type of person can achieve integration at the neglect of their less developed functions. Extraverted persons may tend to emphasize the ministry dimension of religious experience; introverted persons may tend to emphasize the prayer dimension of religious experience.

Prayer, on the other hand, if understood as the exposure of the individual to the action of God for the purpose of achieving the ultimate human satisfaction of loving union with the Divine, takes on differing meanings for individuals with different gifts and orientations. The extraverted person will perhaps be more prone to find God disclosed in the events, persons, and activities in the external world—in social ministry. A more introverted person may find God more meaningfully revealed in the quiet of contemplative prayer. The more integrated person will probably prefer one form of prayer to its opposite but will have designed his or her life so as to encourage Divine disclosures from both the interior and the exterior world.

Finally, a valued acknowledgement of the neglected realm and of the specialized function of the right brain gives meaning to Eastern meditation practices which for many persons in the West seem shrouded in mystery. Body position, mudras, mantras, and mandalas—movement, repeated tones, and geometric forms—facilitate the deautomization of our ordinary consciousness. They enable the individual to disconnect the external functioning of sense perception. They can create the receptive, physiological conditions that can ultimately lead to a surrender by the ego of its conscious controlling action.

One conclusion of this search suggests that to create strict dichotomies between forms of prayer or between spirituality and ministry is to cause human growth to disintegrate. The dichotomous poles need each to be acknowledged, developed, and reconciled. A bi-modal prayer-life would integrate the inner with the outer realm, would integrate contemplative spirituality with active ministries, and would integrate the human person.

Conversion, Liminality, and Stages of Development

The model suggests that growth is similar to the process of conversion. A period of detachment and disintegration is followed by a period of awkward transition and finally by a period of reintegration around a new center of consciousness. These death-rebirth events appear at periods of transition during the life cycle. Jung identifies four major transitions; other theorists concerned with affective, cognitive, or moral development—Erikson, Piaget, Kohlberg, Fowler, for example—or with the life cycle itself—Levinson, Gould, Sheehy, Hall—indicate more specific stages and transitions. The model suggests that transition periods between stages follow the threefold pattern of conversion. Becoming conscious of the awkwardly painful and liminal aspects of the first two periods could engender greater acceptance and patience with ourselves or with others undergoing these experiences.

It also seems that Christian asceticism can be illumined by understanding the "conversion-like" nature of the growth process. Ascetic practices would not be envisioned as morbid denial but rather as a chosen means to growth and new life. By choosing to detach ourselves from our accustomed, comfortable way of doing things, we voluntarily enter the death-rebirth experience. We foster a disintegration process, we embrace the pain and suffer separation so that we can become more profoundly aware of God's presence in our lives—a new center of consciousness.

Sexism, Women's Development, and Wholistic Human Growth

By sexism I mean the typical masculine chauvinistic attitudes, exhibited by persons of both sexes dominated by patriarchal values, and postures taken by some forms of feminism. The former group is very large, including men who espouse the belief of masculine superiority and its associated behavior and women who believe they benefit from the superior position of the male sex. For many persons in this group, their sexism reflects an unexamined, implicit attitude about the nature of human life internalized through cultural conditioning. The latter group is significantly smaller and includes women vividly conscious of masculine oppression in our culture and avowedly determined to redress their grievances in one of two equally sexist ways. The strategy of the first feminist-sexist position is "to fight fire with fire," that is, to surpass men at their own game of exclusively developing rational analytic modes of consciousness and behavior. To buy into this masculine form of sexism is merely to populate the world with more unintegrated, one-sided individuals. The strategy of the second feminist-sexist position argues that "if masculine ways are bad, then feminine ways are good," that enlightened women will follow the path of "this other way." It is a way grounded in experience, in the nature of things; not in abstract principles, not in the head; it is holistic rather than analytic. Such positions may be a necessary initial stance for women who have suffered the oppressive domination of arrogant, self-righteous, ego-inflated men, but it cannot be the ultimate goal of life if we acknowledge the existence of polarity in human life and the need for its reconciliation.

If conceived in a social context including both men and women, the image of the androgyne with developed but reconciled polar opposites provides several options for women who can plan the course of their own development. If women become consciously aware of the need to develop both dimensions of their lives—the extravertedly oriented ego directed way of the left brain and introvertedly oriented receptive way of the right brain—they need not be unduly concerned with which dimension is fostered first. Women initially schooled by the dominant patriarchal values may, at mid-life, become aware of their need to become more actively assertive and personally autonomous. Such women need not abandon their nurturant and receptive skills. Rather they may need only to develop the analytic, logical, organizing skills and the sensitivity to know which mode of conscious behavior is the more appropriate in a given set of circumstances. These women would probably follow the pattern indicated by Jung who suggested that women discover their "animus"—the masculine principle—within themselves which represents the less well developed parts of their psyche. On the other hand, women who during the first half of their lives have succeeded in professional careers may need to discover and to educate the more receptive, relation-seeking, holistic parts of their psyches. While it seems inappropriate to label this the "anima" or feminine principle, it does seem evident that the inner, unconscious, more tender aspect of the psyche is the less developed part. Jung's notion that the "anima" and "animus" are discovered by men and women respectively during mid-life implies that men and women always develop their like-sex characteristics first. This may be the usual case with men; it is probably less often the case with women, especially professionally educated women.

It is interesting to speculate about what the pattern of development might be if we adopted a wholistic model for human growth and were not engulfed like fish swimming in a patriarchal sea. If we were educated to consciously alternate between both modes of conscious behavior during the first half of life, would mid-life crises be so traumatic? Does the psychoanalytic form of therapy which attempts to restore the ego to its center of authority only make sense in a patriarchal society? Does the sex-related language of Jung only apply to persons conditioned by patriarchal values? Might certain aspects of the human potential movement become a part of normal living? Might art and poetry and religion be experienced as part of ordinary life—something ordinary people experience?

Learning Theory, Modes of Inquiry, and Educational Practice

It is interesting to speculate what would happen if the "symbolic thought" of the pre-operational child were not looked upon as primitive, autistic and pathological; if it were encouraged to develop, not at the expense of concrete operational thought, but alternately with it. It is interesting to envision a school curriculum that devoted as much attention to the development of feeling and intuition as it does to reading, writing, and arithmetic, skills all directly related to the left brain's functional specialty.

It would seem that an understanding of bi-modal consciousness could enrich our appreciation of the arts and our understanding of the nature of scientific inquiry. Artists frequently are at a loss for words to describe their creative processes; many scientists, and consumers of science, fail to acknowledge the role of symbol, of creativity, and of imaginative insight, in the development of scientific models. It would seem that educational practice would do well to educate both modes of human consciousness. If we could overcome our fear of the inner human realm, we could educate ourselves to tap the unexplored depths of the human psyche. At the boundary between our known inner world and the unknown we not only discover our limits but we encounter the self-revealing immanent, transcendent other dwelling within us.

AN EPILOGUE

The full moon wanes
        hidden parts emerge.
        The ebbing tide
            reveals gifts
            long submerged.

Colored clouds fade
        mysterious fog
            rains on the earth.
Shadow envelops the world.

In the cave of confusion
        an ego died
            was crucified
            and entombed.
        An inner self rises
            dusty, violent, broken.

An old tomb
        a new womb
        in the Ground of my Being.
A hole impaled
        by Wholeness
        The Hole of Holiness
            The Matrix of
            All Living Things.

The chapters of this essay reflect my personal journey, especially that aspect of my life during which I have traveled the liminal roads from being engulfed in a patriarchal value system to being enlightened by a more wholistic view of life. I have clarified much of the imagery used in the free form verse which began the work. The "matter" of my life, the ground of my being, is that from which the first part of my life was formed. Within the structure of that "stuff" is both a womb and a tomb—the womb and the tomb of both the Self and the ego. The first half of my life was truly an ego-inflated trip, a schizophrenic journey which radically rent my rational conscious world from my sorely neglected interior realm.

Although preceded by some inner dissatisfaction that things were not all well, a request for my resignation came as a sudden abrupt event from without which completely turned my world around. My first response was indeed affective—anger and confusion filled my world. Gradually new imagery began to emerge which seemed to make sense but I could not explain why. Through it I sought to discover and to experience, even to embrace, both the light and dark sides of my interior world. Through more systematic research I have come to discover how these processes fit into a wholistic life, a life informed by faith in the God who is revealed in Jesus and his Spirit. The journey, although painful in many parts, has enabled me to experience myself more wholistically and to envision a more wholistic course for the rest of my life.

NOTES

Chapter I

1. Pierre Teilhard de Chardin, *The Phenomenon of Man* (New York: Harper Colophon Books, 1975).
2. Although I have consulted various works of C. G. Jung and Jungian analysts, the most consistently helpful source has been Ann Belford Ulanov, *The Feminine in Jungian Psychology and in Christian Theology* (Evanston: Northwestern University Press, 1971).
3. Evelyn Underhill, *Mysticism* (New York: Meridian, New American Library, 1974).
4. William Johnston, *Silent Music: The Science of Meditation* (San Francisco: Harper and Row, 1976).

Chapter II

1. Teilhard, *op. cit.*, p. 56.
2. *Ibid.*, pp. 301, 308.
3. *Ibid.*, pp. 60–61, 290, 308.
4. *Ibid.*, pp. 62–66.
5. *Ibid.*, p. 65.
6. *Ibid.*
7. *Ibid.*, pp. 143, 167.
8. Ulanov, *op. cit.*, and also M. Esther Harding, *The Way of All Women* (New York: C. G. Jung Foundation for Analytical Psychology, Inc., 1970), James Hillman, *The Myth of Analysis* (Evanston: Northwestern University Press, 1972), and Marie-Louise von Franz and James Hillman, *Jung's Typology* (Zurich: Spring Publications, 1971)

provide the material for understanding the development of the human psyche.

9. Teilhard, *op. cit.,* pp. 48–49, 71.

10. *Ibid.,* pp. 151–152, 180.

11. *Ibid.,* pp. 167–168.

12. *Ibid.,* pp. 71, 180.

13. *Ibid.,* pp. 148–149, 153, 180.

14. *Ibid.,* p. 221.

15. *Ibid.,* pp. 154–155, 159, 257.

16. *Ibid.,* pp. 155, 172.

17. *Ibid.,* pp. 155–160, 172–173.

18. *Ibid.,* pp. 263–265, and Pierre Teilhard de Chardin, *Human Energy* (London: Collins, 1969), p. 65.

19. Teilhard, *Human Energy,* pp. 65–74.

20. *Ibid.,* p. 57.

21. *Ibid.,* p. 65 and Teilhard, *Phenomenon,* p. 259.

22. Teilhard, *Phenomenon,* pp. 294–299.

23. *Ibid.,* p. 261.

Chapter III

1. Underhill, *op. cit.,* p. 102.

2. *Ibid.,* p. 446.

3. *Ibid.,* pp. 168–170, 446–449.

4. *Ibid.,* pp. 176–177.

5. *Ibid.,* pp. 233–258.

6. *Ibid.,* pp. 418–431.

7. *Ibid.,* pp. 176–177.

8. *Ibid.,* p. 178.

9. *Ibid.,* pp. 216–217.

10. *Ibid.,* p. 401.

11. *Ibid.,* pp. 382–397.

12. Johnston, *op. cit.,* pp. 55–58.

13. *Ibid.,* pp. 68–73.

14. *Ibid.,* pp. 75–78.

15. *Ibid.,* pp. 82–84.

16. *Ibid.,* pp. 86–91.

17. *Ibid.,* p. 110.

18. *Ibid.,* pp. 56–65.

19. *Ibid.,* p. 112.

20. *Ibid.,* pp. 112–117.

21. *Ibid.,* pp. 118–121.

22. Donald L. Gelpi, *Experiencing God* (New York: Paulist Press, 1978), pp. 139–142.

23. Johnston, *op. cit.,* p. 131.

24. *Ibid.*, pp. 143–148.
25. *Ibid.*, p. 148.
26. *Ibid.*, pp. 154–156.
27. *Ibid.*, pp. 157–160.
28. Underhill, *op. cit.*, pp. 95–124.
29. Johnston, *op. cit.*, pp. 75, 157.
30. Underhill, *op. cit.*, p. 444.
31. Johnston, *op. cit.*, p. 83.
32. *Ibid.*, p. 84.
33. Underhill, *op. cit.*, p. 446.
34. Johnston, *op. cit.*, p. 83.
35. Gelpi, *op. cit.*, p. 159, makes a nice distinction between human activity which is natural and that which is gracious. Natural activity neither affirms nor denies the historical self-revelation of God in Jesus and his Spirit. Gracious activity is a response motivated by a positive faith-dependence on the historical self-revelation of God.

Chapter IV

1. Erich Neumann, *The Origin and History of Consciousness* (Princeton: Princeton University Press, 1954), pp. xvi–xix.
2. *Ibid.*, p. xxii.
3. *Ibid.*, pp. 13–16.
4. *Ibid.*, p. 18.
5. *Ibid.*, pp. 18–35.
6. *Ibid.*, pp. 45–101.
7. *Ibid.*, pp. 103–121.
8. *Ibid.*, p. 131.
9. *Ibid.*, pp. 132–151.
10. *Ibid.*, p. 152.
11. *Ibid.*, p. 165.
12. *Ibid.*, pp. 183–185.
13. *Ibid.*, p. 187.
14. *Ibid.*, pp. 189–190.
15. *Ibid.*, pp. 195–203.
16. *Ibid.*, p. 205.
17. *Ibid.*, p. 219.
18. *Ibid.*, p. 42.
19. Erich Neumann, "The Psychological Stages of Feminine Development," in *Spring* (New York: The Analytical Psychology Club, 1959).
20. Donald Gelpi, *op. cit.*, p. 36.
21. *Ibid.*, pp. 173–174.
22. Neumann, *Origin and History of Consciousness*, p. 36.

23. *Ibid.*, p. 205.

24. Gelpi, *op. cit.*, p. 327.

25. Barbara Charlesworth Gelpi, "The Androgyne," in *Women and Analysis* edited by Jean Strouse (New York: Dell Publishing Co., Inc., 1974).

26. June Singer, *Androgyny* (New York: Doubleday, 1976).

27. James Hillman, *The Myth of Analysis* (Evanston: Northwestern University Press, 1972).

Chapter V

1. William James, *Varieties of Religious Experience* (New York: Macmillan Publishing Co., Inc., 1961), p. 305.

2. Robert E. Ornstein, *The Psychology of Consciousness* (New York: Harcourt Brace Jovanovich, Inc., 1977).

3. *Ibid.*, p. 69.

4. *Ibid.*, pp. 46–49.

5. *Ibid.*, p. 57.

6. *Ibid.*, p. 64.

7. *Ibid.*, p. 67.

8. *Ibid.*, pp. 71–72.

9. *Ibid.*, p. 22.

10. David Galin, M.D., "The Two Modes of Consciousness and the Two Halves of the Brain," in *Symposium on Consciousness* (New York: Viking Press, 1974), pp. 30–39.

11. *Ibid.*, pp. 40–41.

12. Ornstein, *op. cit.*, p. 30.

13. Galin, *op. cit.*, p. 42.

14. *Ibid.*, pp. 44–45.

15. Edward C. Whitmont, *The Symbolic Quest* (New York: Harper and Row, 1969), pp. 23–25.

16. Jerome S. Bruner, *On Knowing: Essays for the Left Hand* (New York: Atheneum, 1965), pp. 2–5 and *The Process of Education* (New York: Random House, 1960).

17. Donald Gelpi, *op. cit.*, pp. 94–95 and 240–243.

18. An extended discussion of personality types by Jung himself can be readily obtained in Joseph Campbell, *The Portable Jung* (New York: Penguin Books, 1976), pp. 178–272. Marie-Louise von Franz, "The Inferior Function," in *Jung's Typology* (Zurich: Spring Publications, 1971), pp. 1–72, provides an excellent description of the dynamic relationship among the functions.

19. Galin, *op. cit.*, pp. 40–41.

20. James, *loc. cit.*

Chapter VI

1. Donald Gelpi, *op. cit.*, pp. 64–80.
2. *Ibid.*, pp. 80–94.
3. *Ibid.*, pp. 94–97.

BIBLIOGRAPHY

Bruner, Jerome S. *On Knowing: Essays for the Left Hand.* New York: Atheneum, 1965.

———. *The Process of Education.* New York: Random House, 1960.

Campbell, Joseph. *The Portable Jung.* New York: Penguin Books, 1976.

Galin, M.D., David. "The Two Modes of Consciousness and the Two Halves of the Brain," in *Symposium on Consciousness.* New York: Viking Press, 1974.

Gelpi, Barbara Charlesworth. "The Androgyne," in *Women and Analysis.* Edited by Jean Strouse. New York: Dell Publishing Co., Inc., 1974.

Gelpi, S. J., Donald. *Experiencing God.* New York: Paulist Press, 1978.

Harding, M. Esther. *The Way of All Women.* New York: C. G. Jung Foundation for Analytical Psychology, Inc., 1970.

Hillman, James. *The Myth of Analysis.* Evanston: Northwestern Press, 1972.

James, William. *The Varieties of Religious Experience.* New York: Macmillan Publishing Co., Inc., 1961.

Johnston, S.J., William. *Silent Music: The Science of Meditation.* San Francisco: Harper and Row, 1976.

Neumann, Erich. "The Psychological Stages of Feminine Development" in *Spring.* New York: The Analytical Psychology Club, 1959.

———. *The Origins and History of Consciousness.* Princeton: Princeton University Press, 1954.

Ornstein, Robert E. *The Psychology of Consciousness.* New York: Harcourt Brace Jovanovich, Inc., 1977.

Singer, June. *Androgyny.* New York: Doubleday, 1976.

Teilhard de Chardin, S.J., Pierre. *Human Energy.* London: Collins, 1969.

————. *The Phenomenon of Man.* New York: Harper Colophon Books, 1975.

Ulanov, Ann Belford. *The Feminine in Jungian Psychology and in Christian Theology.* Evanston: Northwestern University Press, 1971.

Underhill, Evelyn. *Mysticism: A Study of the Nature and Development of Man's Spiritual Consciousness.* New York: New American Library, 1974.

von Franz, Marie-Louise and Hillman, James. *Jung's Typology.* Zurich: Spring Publications, 1971.

Whitmont, Edward C. *The Symbolic Quest.* New York: Harper and Row, 1969.